The
10 Best Decisions
Every Parent Can Make

Bill & Pam Farrel

HARVEST HOUSE PUBLISHERS

EUGENE, OREGON

P.S. So...

Published in association with the literary agency of Alive Communications, Inc., 7680 Goddard Street, Suite 200, Colorado Springs, CO 80920

Cover by Left Coast Design, Portland, Oregon

Cover Photo © Teo Lannie / PhotoAlto / Picturequest

THE 10 BEST DECISIONS EVERY PARENT CAN MAKE
Copyright © 2006 by Bill and Pam Farrel
Published by Harvest House Publishers
Eugene, Oregon 97402
www.harvesthousepublishers.com

Library of Congress Cataloging-in-Publication Data
Farrel, Pam, 1959–
    The 10 best decisions every parent can make / Pam Farrel and Bill Farrel.
       p. cm.
    Rev. ed. of: The treasure inside your child / Pam Farrel.
    Includes bibliographical references (p.).
    ISBN-13: 978-0-7369-1709-4 (pbk.)

    1. Parenting—Religious aspects—Christianity. I. Farrel, Bill, 1959–   II. Farrel, Pam, 1959–
    Treasure inside your child. III. Title.
    BV4529.F38   2006
    248.8'45—dc22   2005033859

09 10 11 12 13 14 /BP-CF/ 10 9 8 7 6 5

To our sons, Brock, Zach, and Caleb: You are a blessing! We know you will continue to make great decisions with God's help. Calling you our sons has been and will continue to be a privilege.

To our new daughter-in-law, Hannah: Thank you for deciding to follow God and listen to His call on your life that brought you into our family. You are precious, and we adore you.

To Sheryl and Brian: Thanks for raising such a terrific daughter. And thank you for owning Amazing Grace bookstore, where the kids could meet.

To our nieces and nephews, Bek, Lora, Jake, Owen, Gigi, Brad, Kevin, Jill, and Lindsay: May God continue to lead you to His best for your life.

❧❧❧

For the LORD God is a sun and shield;
the LORD bestows favor and honor;
no good thing does he withhold
from those whose walk is blameless.

PSALM 84:11

Contents

ONE

Decide to Be a Proactive Parent
Envisioning a Legacy Worth Creating

ᷢᷢᷢ

The four of us stood in the church foyer, parents of the bride and groom, reflecting on how fast time flies (when you're having fun?). The day before, the two fathers kidded about the picture for which they would pose. They would turn their pockets inside out and hold the ten-foot-long tuxedo rental receipt for the final picture of the day.

Our firstborn children were now embarking on their adult lives together. Their wedding cost us a bundle, but it provided an opportunity to reflect. We reminisced about their first steps, their first shoes, their first dates, and their first cars. We marveled at all the money we had spent in their lifetimes on clothes, food, makeup, and activities. Our bank accounts would temporarily resemble a black hole, but we had to admit that all our kids are worth every penny we've spent. The value they have added to our lives is a priceless treasure. The braces, the cars, the college books and dorms, and the lessons for musical instruments (long since sold) do have a price tag, but the memories of their lives have become the highlights of ours. All the worries, stresses, and long, hard days of parenting are rewarded in moments like this, the graduation day, the wedding day, and eventually, the first grandchild. It all seems to go so quickly.

The Realities of Parenthood

We have three children. At the time of the writing of this book, Caleb is a freshman in high school, Zach is a university sophomore, and Brock is a 21-year-old newlywed, married to a wonderful, godly wife, Hannah.

I (Pam) vividly remember the birth of our first child, Brock. After months of anticipation, Christmas Day finally arrived—my due date. Because I couldn't travel, my family came to me. All day long they looked at my protruding stomach and waited for labor to magically start. But it didn't. By the end of the day, I had come to grips with my first eye-opening parenting discovery: I am not in control.

Six days later, on New Year's Eve, my contractions came...and came and came. After nearly 20 hours of labor, the nurse announced I was only dilated to one centimeter and the baby was in fetal distress. Brock was ushered into the world by means of an emergency C-section. Eye-opening discoveries two and three: Parenting hurts, and no one can ever explain just how much you will love your child.

My mom had arrived two days before Christmas to help me for two weeks after the baby was born, but Brock's stubbornness about arriving on time had eaten up several of those days. So my wonderful mother, with all her practical wisdom and calm assurance, was whisked out the door and off to the airport just over a week after we brought our new son home. About 2:00 AM that same night Brock woke up ready to eat. Bill had committed to get the baby for these nightly feedings, so he brought Brock to me. I couldn't find a comfortable position to nurse in bed, so I went out to the living room to sit with my small, soft bundle and pray.

"Ah, God, this is exactly how I pictured motherhood. My baby looks so angelic resting on my breast. I'm looking forward to parenting Brock alongside my wonderful husband. He is so wise, so godly, such a good and gentle and handsome man. I hope Brock will look and act just like him. Life is so perfect..."

As I rocked and talked to God, Brock finished nursing and fell asleep in my arms—for a few brief minutes. Then he started to cry. I rocked him and burped him, but he kept crying. I walked with him and sang to him, but he kept crying. I put him in the baby swing, and he cried even louder. I took him back out, and in my heart I shouted to God an order: "God, You control the whole universe, can't You control this baby? Please make him quit crying!"

But Brock kept crying.

I tried giving him a bottle of water, but he kept crying. I walked and I jiggled and I patted, and he kept crying. Finally, I did what only seemed right at a time like this—I began crying also! We were sharing a deep, mother-son bonding moment in the middle of a pitch black room as we sobbed our eyes out. I thought about waking up Bill, but I didn't think he would know what to do—he hadn't even babysat growing up. I thought about calling my mom. I knew she'd know what to do, but it was 4:00 AM. I knew she would be fine if I called, but that would mean I'd have to own up to the fact that *I had no idea what I was doing!*

I walked, patted, and sang every hymn and baby lullaby I could think of. I even made up a lullaby, hoping to get points for creative mothering. He still kept crying. I finally decided to wake up Bill, hoping he would miraculously have some idea of what to do. Unfortunately, he was as clueless as I was. Before this moment, we could never understand how emotions could get away from a person so much that they would shake a baby just to quiet him or her. But now we did understand, and that understanding frightened us. We were exhausted and overwhelmed and committed to somehow learn how to be parents.

Our first decision as parents has to be to *decide to be proactive.*

We didn't have what we needed. We didn't have the answers, the patience, or the wisdom that was now required of us. We needed some help!

I remember my first step toward becoming proactive. I made a plea through tears as I held that tiny, crying baby. "Lord, I know You can make Brock quit crying. You have the power, but I don't think that's what You want here. I admit I don't have a clue. Even though I read parenting books and attended classes for parents of newborns, I still don't know what to do. I've tried everything I know, so I guess I am asking for a miracle. I need Your wisdom. I have none of my own. God, please give me Your wisdom. I'm resting in You. I'm counting on You."

Brock didn't instantly stop crying, but immediately after that prayer I was filled with an unusual peace. Although I didn't have the answer at that moment, I felt assured an answer would come. As I relaxed, my body began to slow to a rhythmic sway. I didn't feel frantic anymore, so my pats on Brock's back gave way to a tender gentle circling motion. In what seemed to me to be a miracle, my son slowly calmed down and fell fast asleep.

We had known intellectually that we could depend on God, that He loved our son even more than we did, but now we were emotionally convinced as well. We decided that day to go to God first when we wondered what to do as parents. We decided to take God up on His offer: "If any of you lacks wisdom, he should ask God, who gives generously to all without finding fault, and it will be given to him" (James 1:5). What a gracious God. We could ask Him anything, and we'd never hear, "What a stupid question!" or "I can't believe you can't figure this one out!"

I have seen Him lead me to hear just the right show on the radio or sit next to just the right mom who had gone through exactly what I was struggling with. He has sent me just the right magazine on just the right day with just the right article in it. Bill and I have read verses in the Bible that seem to pop off the page with just the right perspective. We've remembered just the right story from our own upbringing, and we've had just the right new idea pop into one of our minds at just the right time. The more we committed to prayer, the more we saw God answer.

Father on the Front Lines

This parenting journey was a whole new adventure for me (Bill). I was the youngest of three children in my home, so not only had I never babysat, I never had to take care of a younger brother or sister. I was now thrust into the hot seat of fatherhood. It started out gloriously as the day of Brock's birth provided one dramatic moment after another. Pam told you about the 20-plus hours of labor, but she didn't tell you about my first impression of my son. Brock was experiencing fetal distress because his umbilical chord was bunched up next to his head. Every time Pam had a contraction, Brock's heartbeat would drop. As a result, he was born very blue. I know that all kids are born blue until they take the first breath and oxygen mixes in the blood stream, but my first thought when I saw my oldest son was that *we had given birth to a Smurf!*

To my amazement, he transformed right in front of my eyes. Three snapshots are frozen in time for me from this experience. First, when Brock started crying, his head turned pink, but he still had a blue body! Second, as he continued taking oxygen into his lungs, his torso turned pink also. Now, he had a pink head and a pink torso, but he still had blue arms and legs. Finally, Brock's arms and legs turned pink together, the nurse wrapped him up in a blanket, and she set him in my arms. I remember thinking, "He fits perfectly. This is awesome."

Right then and there, I changed. Up until this moment, I had been afraid and uncertain. I wasn't sure if I had what it took to be a dad and a provider for a family. All that evaporated when I took this new life into my arms. I whispered to God, "Whatever it takes, I am willing to take care of this child. I will work as hard as I need to, sacrifice whatever is required, and invest myself tirelessly. The only problem is that I don't really know what to do. I will supply the willingness. Will you please supply the wisdom?" All this took place on December 31, 1983. I had the opportunity to make my first investment in my son's life the very next day as I introduced him to the world of football on New Year's Day!

We are on a parenting journey. Like you, we are travelers on this road as we look for ways to bring out the best in our children, and we have discovered a map. God's Word and the principles in it can serve us all well. Our hope is that this book will serve as a compass to guide you to the unique treasure that God has prepared for you and your children.

Deliberate parenting begins with a focused pursuit of God's wisdom. The Bible is a treasure map for the proactive parent, and prayer is an inexhaustible connection to the greatest Parent who has ever lived. God will send you positive solutions to negative and not easily understood situations. To succeed on this hunt we must prepare our own hearts to see the treasure in our children.

Desperate Parents Will Pray Desperate Things

Hannah desperately wanted a child. Her husband tried to help with words he thought were encouraging: "Hannah, why are you weeping? Why don't you eat? Why are you downhearted? Don't I mean more to you than ten sons?" (1 Samuel 1:8). That's like asking, "Isn't my love enough?" But it wasn't. Hannah wanted a baby. In her distress, she went to the temple to pray. She didn't know what else to do, so she poured out her heart to God.

She must have been an emotional wreck because when Eli the priest saw her praying, he thought she was drunk. But she wasn't! She was honest, transparent, real, and in real need of an answer from God.

> In bitterness of soul Hannah wept much and prayed to the LORD. And she made a vow, saying, "O LORD Almighty, if you will only look upon your servant's misery and remember me, and not forget your servant but give her a son, then I will give him to the LORD for all the days of his life, and no razor will ever be used on his head."
>
> As she kept on praying to the LORD, Eli observed her mouth. Hannah was praying in her heart, and her lips were moving but her voice was not heard. Eli thought she was drunk and said to her, "How long will you keep on getting drunk? Get rid of your wine."
>
> "Not so, my lord," Hannah replied, "I am a woman who is deeply troubled. I have not been drinking wine or beer; I was pouring out my soul to the LORD. Do not take your servant for a wicked woman; I have been praying here out of my great anguish and grief."
>
> Eli answered, "Go in peace, and may the God of Israel grant you what you have asked of him."
>
> She said, "May your servant find favor in your eyes." Then she went her way and ate something, and her face was no longer downcast.

> Early the next morning they arose and worshiped before the LORD and then went back to their home at Ramah. Elkanah lay with Hannah his wife, and the LORD remembered her. So in the course of time Hannah conceived and gave birth to a son. She named him Samuel, saying, "Because I asked the LORD for him" (1 Samuel 1:10-20).

In her prayer Hannah had promised something every parent should promise—to give our children back to God. We do not own our children. God has lent them to us, entrusted them to us, and our job as parents is to pass on to them God's wisdom, God's perspective, and God's instruction, all the while holding them with an openhanded attitude. This is the first skill that will lead you to God's wisdom. "They are Yours, God. Make me a good steward. Help me love them as You would. Help me parent them as You would. Make me more like You so they can see You and Your will clearly."

Godly Parents Model Integrity

The second skill that will prepare our hearts to understand the map is integrity. Our son Caleb has a keen memory. Anytime we even appear to have forgotten anything, Caleb will say, "You promised!" He knows we only promise if we intend on keeping our word. Because of that, we are very careful with what we have promised.

Hannah promised God she would give her son back to Him to serve in His temple. But think of how she must have felt, how she might have rationalized reneging on her word. She could have argued, "But look at all those other women with all those children. Can't You just use one of theirs?" or "But God, I have only had him for a few years. Can't You wait until he is older?"

But Hannah kept her promise. She was a woman of integrity.

> She said to her husband, "After the boy is weaned, I will take him and present him before the LORD, and he will live there always."
>
> "Do what seems best to you," Elkanah her husband told her. "Stay here until you have weaned him; only may the

LORD make good his word." So the woman stayed at home and nursed her son until she had weaned him.

After he was weaned, she took the boy with her, young as he was, along with a three-year-old bull, an ephah of flour and a skin of wine, and brought him to the house of the LORD at Shiloh. When they had slaughtered the bull, they brought the boy to Eli, and she said to him, "As surely as you live, my lord, I am the woman who stood here beside you praying to the LORD. I prayed for this child, and the LORD has granted me what I asked of him. So now I give him to the Lord. For his whole life he will be given over to the LORD" (1 Samuel 1:22-28).

What was the outcome of Hannah's integrity?

Her son Samuel heard God's clear and personal call to the ministry when he was very young, and he went on to be one of the greatest judges in Israel's history, even being chosen to anoint kings Saul and David.

The best gift Hannah gave her son was the example of integrity.

Character Counts

In parenting, more is caught than taught. The phrase, "Do as I say, not as I do" inevitably falls on deaf ears. For example, did you grow up with a parent who...

- abused drugs or alcohol
- was jailed for breaking a law
- was absent due to workaholism
- abandoned you
- was hooked on pornography
- was physically abusive
- was emotionally or verbally abusive
- was sexually abusive
- was chronically unemployed
- was no longer at home because of divorce

- had an affair
- once walked with God and then left the faith

If any of these events are a part of your background, you will have to replace much of what you caught with new skills that are taught. Take courage! You can't change what happened to you, but you can decide to be proactive and make wise choices to be the best parent possible for your own children. You have a choice. You can be like Timothy's mother and grandmother, whom the apostle Paul commended for passing the baton of faith well: "I have been reminded of your sincere faith, which first lived in your grandmother Lois and in your mother Eunice and, I am persuaded, now lives in you also" (2 Timothy 1:5).

Timothy, even as a youth, was a godly leader. He had a head start because his mother decided to be proactive. You can choose what you will pass on as a legacy. It can be dysfunction and sin or health and holiness. Exodus 34:7 (KJV) describes the effect of dysfunction: "Keeping mercy for thousands, forgiving iniquity and transgression and sin, and that will by no means clear the guilty; visiting the iniquity of the fathers upon the children, and upon the children's children, unto the third and to the fourth generation."

This doesn't mean that God holds the sin of a grandparent against a grandchild yet unborn. Rather, it is a statement of fact: Left unchecked, the sins of the father will be visited upon generation after generation. The reason this is true is that unhealthy families express their love in unhealthy ways: yelling, chaos, one dramatic event after another, violence, rejection, and so on. Children who see Dad hit Mom and then make up with roses will learn that love and pain go hand in hand. Unless they deliberately retrain themselves, they will choose to marry a person who will help them reestablish the pattern—even learning behavior patterns to push a person to say or do things that will feel painful. It is a horrible cycle, but we see it in marriages and families all around us. Sin looks normal when it is repeated generation after generation. That's why we find generation after generation of welfare mothers. Girls who had fathers who abused alcohol, drugs, and tobacco will often marry men who abuse. Patterns of lying, cheating, stealing, and divorce will show up in branch after branch of the family tree.

But you can also break that cycle and establish healthy patterns. A psalmist declares, "We will not hide them from their children; we will tell the next generation the praiseworthy deeds of the LORD, his power, and the wonders he has done…to teach their children, so the next generation would know them, even the children yet to be born, and they in turn would tell their children" (Psalm 78:4-6).

That is why you can also see generation after generation of pastors, missionaries, Christian leaders, and strong godly families. In my travels, I (Pam) have the privilege of meeting children and grandchildren of spiritual leaders whom I have looked up to because of their writings, their radio ministries, and their biographies. When I ask these younger generations what growing up in their family was like, they often make statements like these: "It was normal to obey God," or "I can never remember a crisis when our whole family didn't pray or a Christmas where we didn't read the Christmas story." One woman, who was the sixth generation to be in full-time ministry, said, "I cannot imagine not having the strength of my heritage. When I encounter a problem in ministry, I can call my parents, grandparents, aunts, uncles, brothers…I have so many who will pray for me and give me godly counsel."

This kind of heritage provides great strength, and it can begin with you! What legacy do you want to leave? What heritage do you want to build?

A Redeemer and a Rebuilder

As a parent, you can repent and rebuild. At any moment you can decide to be a positive, proactive parent. I (Pam) had a creative, goal-setting, nurturing mother. I believe she absorbed much of the trauma of our home. She often stood between me and the wrath and anger of my alcoholic father. When I came home from dates, I remember praying, begging God to not let my dad be passed out on the front lawn in his underwear, in an angry rage, or worse—suicidal.

When I was a preschooler, my mother had a friend named Kathy who was a secretary of a little church in our small town. Mom noticed that Kathy had what she wanted—peace, joy, and patience. The fruit of the spirit emanated from Kathy's life. My mother began to attend

Kathy's church, and she always took my brother, my sister, and me to Sunday school. Mom would then go home, but I would beg to stay for "big church" (the worship service). God remade my life and my mom's simultaneously.

Mom constantly asked spiritual questions because her parents never taught her to think biblically. She volunteered to help in children's ministry, but because she only had questions and not many answers, the leaders put her in charge of crafts. So Mom and I made our share of Ivory soap Bibles and Popsicle stick crosses.

That beautiful little sanctuary was always lit up with the colored rays shining through its stained glass windows. I felt safe there. In Sunday school I earned a little white cross that glowed in the dark for memorizing the Twenty-third Psalm. On it was printed, "He Lives." One night when I was just eight, as my dad raged and my mom tried to talk him down, I was lying on my bed, looking up at that little cross glowing in the dark. I prayed, "God, at church they tell me You had the power to rise from the dead. I believe You have the power to do anything. When I grow up, I don't want to live in a house like this with all this fighting. I want to live in a house filled with love."

Shortly after that I was trying to earn a place on the quiz team at church. I always tried to earn any award I could because I thought that might make Dad happy and he might show me he loved me. I was memorizing Matthew 5–7 when I came across Matthew 7:7: "Ask and it will be given to you; seek and you will find; knock and the door will be opened to you." There, sitting on my bed, I prayed "God, does this mean if I ask You to come into my life, You will? Please come into my life and be my Best Friend, my Savior, and my Lord."

I believe He met me there that day.

He began to transform me from the inside out. I went from a sullen child who cried at the drop of a hat to a happy, carefree little girl. My circumstances didn't change—God was changing me. And at the same time, God was changing my mother.

God was carrying out His promise to be a Father to the fatherless (Psalm 68:5) to both Mom and me. God had a lot to remake in me: fear of rejection, fear of failure, and fear of men. And I could easily fall into controlling patterns because the home I grew up in felt out of control.

As a teen I even went my own way for a while. However, as I continued to look to God as my Father, He faithfully continued to work with me. God led me to forgive my father, to look at my own weaknesses, and then as a young adult to look to Him as my strength. God got my full attention and helped me reevaluate all of my life—the way I chose men, the way I made decisions, how I dressed, and what activities I partook in. This new process freed me to choose a godly man about a year later. Our relationship and our family are dramatically different from the home I grew up in. And because my mother also surrendered to Christ, the older I grew, the wiser she was becoming. Christ broke the patterns of sin and dysfunction as Mom and I continued to look to Him and not to our own background to guide us. My own mother is now one of the strongest and most positive and spiritually attuned voices in our own children's lives.

It's a Process

As a young mother, I continued to ask God to point out any unhealthy traits, any blind spots I might have because of the way I was raised. At that time, I felt a need to keep a perfect home, and I found myself spending all day every day picking up after my children, getting very little of anything else done, and feeling more and more resentful. Anger was always boiling right under the surface. Then one day in a quiet time, God pointed out that my resentment and anger would make my children feel they had to be perfect and set them up for rebellion against me and Him. I made some key decisions to be proactive and to become aware of and break unhealthy relationship patterns. These are a few of those early proactive steps:

- Put God first. I began to give Him the first 20 minutes of each day. I knew only He could keep my perspective and expectations realistic.

- Whisper instead of yell when frustrated. When I felt anger, I immediately took that anger to Jesus and asked, "What is the underlying fear?" Anger is just a symptom of a deeper issue—what is the issue?

- Make the home a safe place, not a showplace. This one was especially difficult. I wanted my family to look forward to coming home and having friends over. I wanted to use our home for ministry, but crowds can bring chaos—or at least clutter. I chose to only clean up first thing in the morning, right before dinner (sometimes during kids' naps but more often a few minutes before Bill arrived home), and at bedtime. This made for happier children and a mom with healthier interests. I gained time for Bible study, friendships, art, exercise, and education.

- Play a mental a tape of truth—phrases of wisdom and portions of verses that give clarity when old patterns of control threaten the home front. I would tell myself things like, "Lighten up and live life. A quiet answer turns away wrath. The fruit of the spirit is love, joy, peace, patience…and self-control." I found if I had Christian radio or music on all day, we all had better days.

We know God can heal any trauma you or your child may have gone through, but the process requires *work*. As a part of my (Pam's) healing, I read many books, I was discipled and mentored, I sought out good counsel, and I spent nearly two years of my quiet times researching who God was so I could again see Him clearly and receive all that my heavenly Father had for me. God is continually pulling out issues from the closets of my life and then graciously saying, "Okay, Pam, now let's work on repairing this one."

God might open the closet of your life while you read this book. As you learn tools to unlock the treasure in your son or daughter, you might come to grips with some of the shortcomings of your family of origin. Give those hurts to God. He can help you proactively create a new family that reflects all that He has to offer.

I Know and God Knows

When I was first pregnant, even the first day Bill and I discovered I was to have a baby, we would lie in bed, and Bill would place his hand on mine. Then he placed both our hands on my stomach, and we'd pray. We prayed all the typical prayers first-time parents might pray: "Please make the baby healthy…help us be good parents…help this child make a difference in this world." But Bill and I also prayed and asked God big things for our child:

"God, give him or her the faith of a Daniel or a Joseph. Give him or her the courage to stand for You—even the courage to stand alone for You. Make him or her a strong witness of light in this dark world. May many come to know You personally because of the life of this little one."

God answered our prayer over and over. When Brock was a high school sophomore, I (Pam) drove into the school parking lot to pick him up after football practice. It was already dark, and all the players were off the field—everyone except my son, who was putting equipment away. I was in a rush, so I ran to the field. "Brock, honey, I'm in a hurry…"

"Okay, Mom, but I have to do repos." (Repos are grueling exercises football players have to do when they have done something wrong.)

"Why?" I asked. "You *never* have to do repos."

"I didn't send my fund-raising letters," he replied.

"They're sitting on my desk. They're all done; I just have to get stamps for them."

"Yeah, but they aren't sent."

I felt bad for him, but I knew he was right.

I walked back up to the locker room. Brock's teammates were starting to come out.

"Hey, Mrs. Farrel—where's Brock?"

I repeated the story to them. One said, "Man, I didn't send my beg letters either. But coach doesn't know that—and all the coaches are gone. No one would know."

Just then, Brock walked up and heard the conversation. "I'd know, and God knows." His choosing to be a person of integrity was a witness to his friends that day and warmed my heart.

Integrity is a key goal of parenting. We want our children to be authentic, upstanding, moral leaders of their generation. Sometimes God encourages parents by letting them see a glimpse of the fruit of their labors. That's what He did for me that day outside the locker room. But the biggest thrill comes when we pass the baton of faith securely into the hand of the next generation.

By far, the crowning moment we have experienced as parents was Brock and Hannah's wedding ceremony. As Bill officiated at the ceremony and led them through their traditional vows, our hearts smiled. But the opening lines of their personal vows pushed the moment over the top. To hear our son commit his life and heart was a joy, but our hearts overflowed when we heard our precious new daughter-in-law begin her vows with, "Brock, when I look at you, I see a godly man. You are full of integrity and brilliant beyond words..." Those are the days parents wait for and long for, so hang in there—God has some special days waiting for you.

.

Decision Point:
Be a Proactive Parent

We tend to repeat family patterns; sometimes this is good, sometimes it is not. Take inventory of your families of origin. Each of you (Mom and Dad) write three lists:

1. What parts of your own heritage do you want to repeat and reinforce?

2. What family patterns did you grow up with that you want to replace?

3. How will you work to replace them? What are some ways you can begin a new legacy?

Compare notes and talk about the top three priorities you agree on and how you will make sure your family creates and follows through on a proactive plan to achieve them.

① • Emphasis on family + friends, not on "stuff"
• Family vacations

② • Poor communication
• Avoiding problems by pretending they don't exist instead of dealing with them.

③ • Model good communication style
• Family Therapy
• Family Meetings

TWO

Decide to Be Consistent
Helping Kids to Not Settle for Less

༺༺༺

I (Pam) was a chaperone on Zachery's eighth-grade trip to the Mother Lode country. We spent an afternoon panning for gold—in the rain. The air was cold, and the water in the river felt as though the ice had been chipped off so we could dip our pans in it. We heard how miners would wade, sometimes up to their waists, in the frigid water to find a place that had yet to be panned. It was a laborious process. Scoop up a bunch of bedrock, swirl it around in the pan just right so the bigger rocks washed off and the smaller stayed, add water, and swish over and over and over again until only the smallest of pebbles—and hopefully nuggets of gold—remained. Then, if they were fortunate enough to find any gold nuggets, they had to take them sometimes a great distance to have them weighed.

They could trade them for money, or they could become a gold-smith, who would heat up the gold, melting it until the dross or impurities would rise to the surface and then scraping them off. They repeated this process over and over until they could see their own reflection in the pure gold. The entire process, from panning to purification, was arduous, time-consuming, and backbreaking—just as parenting is a time-consuming and often heart-wrenching task. But the results are the same. Nothing feels more rewarding than to shout, "Eureka! I've found pure gold!"

Children are innocent, but they come to us with a bent for bad. Think not?

> A pastor is walking down the street one day when he notices a very small boy trying to press a doorbell on a house across the street. However, the boy is very small, and the doorbell is too high for him to reach. After watching the boy's efforts for some time, the pastor steps smartly across the street, walks up behind the little fellow, and placing his hand kindly on the child's shoulder, leans over and gives the doorbell a solid ring. Crouching down to the child's level, the pastor smiles benevolently and asks, "And now what, my little man?"
>
> To which the boy replies, "Now we run!"

We are sure you didn't have to teach your two-year-old to scream, "No!" or "Mine!" We all have an innate tendency to be selfish. The Bible is clear: "All have sinned" (Romans 3:23). No one has to teach a child to be selfish—that comes prepackaged. In our years of ministering to children, teens, and their families, we have observed five traits that can lead children to destruction. Every child we have ever met has at least one and some have more than that. These traits must be minimized in order for your child to discover and then live out the God-given treasure and calling He has planned. One of our main jobs as parents is to heat up life so that the dross of our children's negative bents can rise to the surface and be removed. To do this we have to make a tough call: *Decide to be consistent.*

We have to outlast, outthink, and outmaneuver our children and their inborn bent to foolishness. I (Bill) often encourage parents by saying, "Our children's full-time job is to be kids. They probably stay up nights thinking of ways to get around the system. We as parents have jobs, family responsibilities, and tasks to attend to at home, at work, in the community, and in the church. Kids have more time to think of creative ways to disobey!" We need to decide to discipline and train our kids consistently when we are tired, when we are preoccupied, when we are frustrated, when we would rather be relaxing, or when we are flat-out angry at them.

The five negative traits that entrap individuals and distract them from their God-given course in life are sensuality, rebellion, shortsightedness, laziness, and plain ol' selfishness. These character flaws can contaminate the treasure inside your child.

Sensuality

Samson was special from the womb. He took a Nazirite vow, which set him apart as a holy leader. But he had a fatal flaw. In Judges 14:1-3, we see a snapshot of his sensual side.

> Samson went down to Timnah and saw there a young Philistine woman. When he returned, he said to his father and mother, "I have seen a Philistine woman in Timnah; now get her for me as my wife."
>
> His father and mother replied, "Isn't there an acceptable woman among your relatives or among all our people? Must you go to the uncircumcised Philistines to get a wife?"
>
> But Samson said to his father, "Get her for me. She's the right one for me."

Judges 16:1 also indicates that Samson had difficulty with his sensuality, "One day Samson went to Gaza, where he saw a prostitute. He went in to spend the night with her."

You may be familiar with Delilah, the beautiful woman who used her sensuality and beauty to pry the secret to Samson's strength from him. Repeatedly Delilah asked Samson the secret to his strength, and he made up answers. Then she would yell, "The Philistines are upon you!" Suddenly soldiers in waiting would try to capture Samson, the strongest man in the nation.

Logic would say, "Samson, get out of there. This woman is no good for you! She's using you! She's willing to sell you out!" But he was ensnared by his own sensual sin. He was addicted to sensuality even at the risk of his own life. Delilah finally pulled the secret to his strength out of him. One fateful evening she cut his hair, and his strength diminished. He was bound and then pitifully blinded.

Take note of your child's interest in the opposite sex. How much does he or she focus on body parts? How does he or she respond to sexually slanted commercials and print ads? Undue interest at a young age is often a flashing warning light.

Because of our position in the church, we see many accidents waiting to happen. On more than one occasion, we have observed eight- and nine-year-old girls wanting to wear makeup, dress provocatively, and place themselves in inappropriate positions with older boys and grown men. A resounding alarm should ring if you see a preteen or young teen sitting on laps, rubbing her body against boys and men, or dressing to arouse. Is your preadolescent son overly interested in the ego-stroking attention of the opposite sex at the sacrifice of other, more vital interests?

If your preteens or teens are losing their direction or purpose, take heed of this serious warning. One teen told us, "This guy at school came right up to me and said, 'Do you want to have sex?' I don't even know him! I know I should be revolted, but something in me wished I could say yes. I liked that he was attracted to me." However, regardless of feelings, the truth is that those who are unwilling to rein in their sensual side will eventually live out the painful consequences of their choices.

Watch how your son responds to ads for underwear or bathing suits, or to cheerleaders on TV. Notice if your daughter longs for overstimulation of her senses. If your kids are caught up in themes that are not age-appropriate, or if they long to have their body always feel good, consider ways to better channel that energy into creativite interests like art, music, or athletics.

Rebellion

Some of the hardest children to parent are the rebellious ones. First Samuel 2:12-16 gives an example of a godly leader who raised his children to know right from wrong, but the sons didn't want to do what was right!

Eli's sons were wicked men; they had no regard for the LORD. Now it was the practice of the priests with the people that whenever anyone offered a sacrifice and while the meat was being boiled, the servant of the priest would come with a three-pronged fork in his hand. He would plunge it into the pan or kettle or caldron or pot, and the priest would take for himself whatever the fork brought up. This is how they treated all the Israelites who came to Shiloh. But even before the fat was burned, the servant of the priest would come and say to the man who was sacrificing, "Give the priest some meat to roast; he won't accept boiled meat from you, but only raw."

If the man said to him, "Let the fat be burned up first, and then take whatever you want," the servant would then answer, "No, hand it over now; if you don't, I'll take it by force."

Rebellious kids have a bent toward evil. They sometimes dabble in Satanism, they can lie to your face, and they may boldly disrespect authority or be passive-aggressive, telling you what you want to hear and then doing the opposite. They often show signs of violence early in life. They may torture animals, treat peers cruelly, or say hateful things. Every child will have periods in his or her life when disobedience is close to the surface, but the rebellious child will display a consistent pattern of being disobedient and argumentative.

Rebellious kids need to know you are tough enough to take them. This refers to consistency in discipline and a calm reassurance that God will disclose their sins and wrongdoings early.

Josh McDowell, teen-parent relationship specialist, says, "Rules without relationship lead to rebellion." Go overboard to build relationships with children who have a bent toward wrong. Ask them to tell you when they are feeling like disobeying. Reward their honesty, but insist they take out the trash or do the dishes. Don't let them replace rebellion with manipulation!

Share some of your own childhood misdeeds with your rebellious child—especially if you suffered negative consequences!

When I (Bill) was five years old, my parents hired a babysitter to watch my sister, my brother, and me for a day. They had to be gone from early in the morning until late at night, so they had a teenager take care of us. She was less than patient with us and not very interested in spending the day with three young, nosey kids. She told my brother and me that we had to spend the day outside. She even locked the door to make sure we didn't come inside. Fortunately, we lived in a very safe neighborhood, so I found a friend of mine, and we went exploring.

We discovered a grove of trees that, in our imagination, was a hideout for secret agents. Then we found a pile of old tires, siding from a house, and various broken tractor parts. In the midst of the pile we also found a book of matches, and boy, were we excited. Imagining the fun we could have, we began to case the neighborhood.

The field next to my house was dry, and I told my friend I was going to light the grass and immediately stomp it out. He, of course, thought it was a great idea because I was starting the fire. Sure enough, I touched the match to the grass and immediately stomped on the area. To my satisfaction, the fire went out and all was well. But this caused my confidence level to rise to dangerous levels, and I said to my friend, "This time, I'm going to light the grass, count to three, and then stomp the fire out." With his enthusiastic support, I lit the grass, patiently counted to three and stomped as hard as I could. Instead of going out, the fire jumped! What I thought would be a quick thrill as I smothered the fire turned into three fires. I tried to stomp on two of them, but that only served to spread the fire farther. By this time, the situation was out of my control. I ran home, crying and scared.

I pounded on the door of my house, and the babysitter screamed at me from the other side. When I told her about the fire, she ran out and saw the flames spreading quickly. She frantically ran back into the house and called the fire department. To make a long story short, the babysitter doused the fence behind our house so it would not burn while the fire truck arrived and put out the grass fire. I was greatly relieved that the firefighters were able to tame this fire without any loss to houses. They wrapped up their work, loaded the hoses on the truck, and tried to back out of the field—only to bury the back wheels in the soft dirt. They had to call a second truck to come tow them out!

By this time, I was ready to crawl into a hole. I will never forget the conversation I had with my parents that night.

"Bill, did you start the fire in the field behind our house?"

No answer from me.

Again, "Bill, you need to tell us if you are the one who started the fire."

"Will I get in trouble if I say I did?" Isn't that a silly response? Of course, my parents knew I was guilty. If they had any doubt before this statement, they were certain now! To their credit, they handled the whole thing with grace and encouragement even though I was on restriction for quite a while. I hated telling my kids that story, especially when they got a huge laugh out of it and said, "You started a fire, Dad? Even we know better than that!"

Shortsightedness

Genesis 25:29-34 shares a story of one very shortsighted choice:

> Once when Jacob was cooking some stew, Esau came in from the open country, famished. He said to Jacob, "Quick, let me have some of that red stew! I'm famished!" (That is why he was also called Edom.)
>
> Jacob replied, "First sell me your birthright."
>
> "Look, I am about to die," Esau said. "What good is the birthright to me?" But Jacob said, "Swear to me first." So he swore an oath to him, selling his birthright to Jacob. Then Jacob gave Esau some bread and some lentil stew. He ate and drank, and then got up and left. So Esau despised his birthright.

Esau had the world by the tail. He was to be the leader of his family, which would grow into a powerful tribe. But he was hungry, so to meet a short-term desire, he gave away the most valuable asset he owned— his birthright.

Kids just don't think life through. A shortsighted teen will bring a knife to a zero-tolerance school just to show his friends how cool it is. A shortsighted child will wander off because he wants to see what is on the other side of the hill. A shortsighted boy is angry, so he slugs his friend, expelling himself from school. A shortsighted girl may go off with friends without calling home because she never considered that others might worry. These kids aren't manipulative or rebellious; they just act without thinking at times. They don't recognize the long-term results of their actions.

Trent (not his real name) was bright, spontaneous, and decisive. Some might even say he was rash. He usually got in trouble for not coming home on time, not calling home if plans changed, or making some risky choice when he was away from his parents. He usually just answered, "Why are you making such a big deal out of this?" He had a hard time seeing why all of life had to be so well thought-out.

In youth group, I (Bill) pulled him aside after class. "Trent, you're a natural leader. The way you act is the way the class acts. If you are involved and cooperative, so are they. If you are out of control, so is the class. God has given you a gift, and I need your help."

Trent responded, "Why does it have to be that way? It's not fair. What if I don't want to lead?"

"It's in your DNA," I replied. "You just have to decide how you're going to use the gift God has given you."

One day at a high school football game, he saw a girl who was cornered and harassed by a group of boys. He ran by numerous coaches, security guards, parents, and teachers to get a friend's pellet gun from his car. Armed and impetuous, he went to confront the thugs. Seeing Trent pull out the gun, the security patrol tackled Trent to the ground instead of going after the group that had been accosting the girl!

The school had a zero tolerance rule, so Trent, a talented athlete, was suspended from the team and the school, and he lost his ability to play sports. Trent's shortsighted solution to the problem cost him dearly.

Laziness

Years ago, a young man named Jerry began attending our church. He was homeless and had a history of drug use (though he claimed he was currently clean), and Bill was helping him get into a long-term rehabilitation program. We talked with our kids about letting him spend a night or two at our house. Brock volunteered to give up his room and his bed.

Program after program was full, and Bill put Jerry's name on waiting list after waiting list. He didn't have a job, so we made a contract he was to abide by while he stayed with us. Just like any member of the family, he would have chores. But we soon saw that our seven- and nine-year-old children worked Jerry under the table! I (Pam) had to constantly get him up off the sofa, remind him to finish tasks, and urge him to keep working toward his simple goals. Jerry was smart—at one time he had an academic scholarship for college. But because of his laziness, he lost that scholarship, he lost job after job, and he was kicked out of one friend's home after another.

One day he asked me if he could use my bike to ride to a friend's and pick up some of his belongings. I let him, encouraged that Jerry was actually showing some motivation. But he didn't come home that night. I thought we'd never see him again, but we did. The next day he came walking in—minus my bike. Jerry said he fell asleep at his friend's house while his friend stole my bike and sold it for drugs. Jerry slept on the floor of our church that night, not in Brock's bed. I would not reward his laziness. The next day, Bill drove him four hours to a rehabilitation program.

If laziness is your child's Achilles' heel, divide chores into small parts and attach a reward to each part. Celebrate each completed math problem with an M&M. Offer phone privileges after the kids make their beds or clean their rooms. Write each chore on a separate Post-it note, line the notes across the TV, and leave the TV off until all the chores are completed and the notes are gone.

Selfishness

The final negative trait that can sidetrack kids is one we all battle: selfishness. We all wish the world revolved around us! We witnessed a vivid example of this at a dinner party. When the dialogue drifted away from one young girl, she lifted her hands, clapped them to gain everyone's attention, and pointing at herself, said, "People, people! Focus, focus! Back to me!"

Most people are not this blatant, but selfish attitudes are prevalent in children. Instead of becoming short-tempered, ask your teens how the people around them are feeling. Ask your kids who Jesus would want them to take care of first. Help them learn to look at others with biblical priorities, like giving preference to the elderly, the weak, the infirm. Help your younger children remember that on certain days, others are given preference: Birthday parties honor the birthday boy or girl, and anniversaries are for married couples. Children need to learn that a family is a team. Children will not reach their full potential if the family revolves around them. Instead, raise your children in a Christ-centered family and follow His model in Philippians 2: "Consider others better than yourselves."

Turning Things Around

How can a parent work to eliminate the negative and accentuate the positive? *Discipline.* What is discipline?

Let's look to God's Word and see what principles we can find:

- "He will die for lack of discipline, led astray by his own great folly" (Proverbs 5:23). If a parent does not discipline, a child is likely to suffer even worse consequences.

- "Discipline your son, and he will give you peace; he will bring delight to your soul" (Proverbs 29:17). A disciplined child will give you peace and bring delight to you.

- "'I am with you and will save you,' declares the LORD…'I will discipline you but only with justice; I will not let you go entirely unpunished'" (Jeremiah 30:11). God disciplines with justice. He doesn't let wrong go unpunished, but neither is He unfair.

- "No discipline seems pleasant at the time, but painful. Later on, however, it produces a harvest of righteousness and peace for those who have been trained by it" (Hebrews 12:11). Giving or receiving discipline will not feel pleasant, but the outcome of righteous living and peace will feel good.

- "Those whom I love I rebuke and discipline. So be earnest, and repent" (Revelation 3:19). The right response to discipline will be a desire to earnestly obey and a repentant heart.

First Things First

From these verses, one can conclude that discipline is necessary and has a positive outcome. Let's look briefly at some specific components of appropriate discipline:

Training first. We must never punish for something the person didn't know was wrong. To do so would be unjust, and God's model is discipline that is just. Irresponsibility should not be punished unless it is deliberate and defiant. Children are naturally clumsy and immature. This is the very reason they need to be trained and instructed by adults. A child should never be made to feel guilty for being a child, and yet too often parents use discipline to respond to spilled milk.

The punishment should fit the offense. A small infraction should be met with a small form of correction. A big wrongdoing should be met with a more stringent form of correction.

A person worthy of honor should give the discipline. The parent who was there at the time of the infraction is best. And your kids will probably receive discipline better if you are living according to God's principles yourself.

Discipline includes physical correction. Scripture permits and even recommends physical punishment.

Correct in control. No punishment, correction, or discipline should ever be given in anger.

The Controversy Continues

To spank or not to spank? Good parents line up on both sides of this issue, and so do bad parents. People's emotions often run high when discussing spanking. No loving person would ever want a child to be abused, but in the same way, no loving person would let children be ruled by their own whims. A swing of the pendulum in either direction is off balance.

Regardless of the form of discipline we use, the way we use it and why is what matters. We prayed about and discussed all forms of discipline before our first baby was born. We decided we would never spank in anger, and we'd never hurl cutting words or dole out consequences if we were angry. We'd pray and make sure our emotions were in check and settled first. We both had grown up with parents who cut to the quick with hurtful words. Hurtful words spoken in anger cause damage rather than correction. We agreed to take words like *stupid* and all its synonyms out of our vocabulary. We made a commitment to use corporal punishment (spanking) for a very limited number of infractions.

As we looked at the teens in our youth group, the kids who were excelling all respected their parents' authority. They had a deep level of trust for their parents' wisdom even when they disagreed with the punishment at the time. We conducted an informal survey. All of the kids who were excelling as teens had been spanked at least a few times during their preschool years, and a few up until about first or second grade. Bill and I decided we wanted to protect our children from worse consequences by using spanking to mark a few key boundaries.

When our boys were toddlers and preschoolers and they did something that might endanger their lives or the lives of their siblings, they received a spanking. For example, running into the street or playing with matches was an offense that called for corporal punishment.

The other offense we punished with spanking was flat-out defiance. This was not simple disobedience but rather included insolent attitudes and words. We knew we had to win the battle of respect when they were four, or we'd never win it at fourteen.

When Brock gradated from high school, we asked him to preach on graduation Sunday. To prepare for the message, we asked him, "We know we were not perfect parents, but of all the things we did, what do you see as the three most important things we did that helped you turn out so well?"

Brock replied, "First, you spanked. You disciplined us—and you were consistent. If you said something, I knew you meant it. Because you disciplined me, I have self-discipline. I go to school with a whole lot of kids who have no inner compass because they were never taught any discipline." Self-discipline was the root of all Brock's successes.

"Second, you prayed for me. Those Moms In Touch prayers in high school felt like a force field of protection. Satan couldn't get to me because you prayed and asked others to pray too.

"Third, you helped me find God's dreams for my life, and then you helped me achieve those dreams."

Someday your 18-year-olds may thank you for disciplining them when they were young.

When Brock was about two, we went to visit my brother and sister-in-law, Bret and Erin, along with their brand-new baby. An old wood stove was the sole heat source in their historic farmhouse. We showed Brock the wood stove and told him not to touch it because it would burn him. Then we told him not to run near it so he wouldn't fall into it. We also asked him to keep his voice down when the baby was sleeping. A few hours later, Brock was running laps and yelling at the top of his lungs as the baby was being rocked near the fireplace. Erin was trying to get the baby to sleep so we could all eat lunch. We asked Brock to stop running. He ran. I (Pam) took him in my arms and whispered, "Brock, come with me." We went around the corner for privacy, and I whispered to him as I tilted his face up toward mine, "Brock, we asked you to stop running because you might fall into the woodstove and get burned. And we asked you to be quiet and not yell. Do you understand?" He nodded yes.

"Okay. Now you tell me—what two things am I asking you to do?"

"Don't run. Don't yell."

"That's correct. Brock, if you disobey these, you will get a spanking. Do you understand?"

He nodded yes.

"What will happen if you yell or run?"

"Spankin'?"

"That's right. Now, you may go play quietly with your books and toys."

Within a few minutes, Brock was running and screaming through the living room. Bill caught him as he ran the next lap through and marched him into an empty office nearby.

"Brock, do you know why we are in here?"

"Spankin'?"

"That's right. Do you know why?"

"I ran and yelled."

"That's right. Would you like to tell God you are sorry?"

Brock prayed a contrite prayer of confession then looked up and said, "Now Daddy, pleeze spank me."

Bill gave one swat across a well-padded training-pant bottom. Brock looked up and said, "Thanks, Dad, I needed that."

Kids may not thank you now for being consistent in discipline and following through, but eventually they will.

Combining Discipline

I have found that the more strong willed the child is, the more creative and layered your discipline will need to be. You will need to attack a sinful pattern of disobedience from all sides.

When Zach was four, we were building a new home. The house had been framed and the roof was on, but the walls had no siding or Sheetrock. Zach discovered an ice chest full of soda, chocolate, and other goodies for the volunteer workers. He would play for a while, and then he would sneak in and look around for witnesses. Thinking he saw none, he'd grab some goodies and flee. We spotted his antics and forbade him from having any more before dinner. Then we saw him sneak in again when we were working in the next room (Zach somehow thought that we couldn't see him through the stud walls!).

He had the ice chest open. "Zach, get out of there right now!" I (Pam) said.

He had a new ring of chocolate around his mouth. I had just moments before wiped dirt and chocolate grime from his face. So I asked, "Zach, did you get more goodies out of the ice chest?"

His cheeks were too stuffed with chocolate to respond, so he shook his head no.

"Zach, tell me the truth. Did you eat more chocolate after I told you not to?"

Again he shook his head no and then tried to swallow all the chocolate in his little mouth.

"Zach, if you tell me the truth, you won't get in as much trouble as you will if you lie to me. Did you eat more chocolate?"

Zach shook his head no. In fact, his whole body shook in a back and forth!

Bill stepped in. "Son, your mother and I saw you take the chocolate just now. Give it up. Own up to what you've done, and it'll be better for you."

Again Zach shook his body as if to say no.

That was enough for me. "Zach, because you disobeyed and then lied, Mommy has to spank you."

I took him to another room and prayed with him, giving him one last chance to repent. Again, he defiantly shook his body. I then gave one swat to his bottom. I looked him eye to eye.

"Zach, Mommy loves you, but she has to be able to trust you. I need you to tell me the truth. Did you take more chocolate?"

This time he shouted no and stomped his little foot.

"Zach, I have to spank you for lying. People can't trust you when they don't know if you are lying or telling the truth. Did you take the chocolate?"

"No!" he shouted in my face so loudly I could smell his chocolate breath!

"Zach, because you are lying to me, I have to spank you." Again I swatted his little bottom.

Bill tried to coerce a confession out of him. Then I tried again. Over and over we ask and pleaded with him to tell the truth. We prayed with him, hoping God's Spirit would help work on his stony little heart. Each time he lied. We knew spanking was not getting through to him. He was determined to outlast us.

Finally, I carried him to the small travel trailer we had on the property. I sat him on the bed and said, "Zach, we all saw what you did. We also know that you are lying about it. You will stay here and think about what happens when you lie." I told him the story of the boy who cried wolf and that when the real wolf came no one believed him. Then I reminded him of his Pinocchio book—that Pinocchio's nose grew every time he lied. I said, "Your nose would be out to here, son, if that were a true story, but it is just make-believe. But this is real, and we can't trust you when you lie. So you'll have to stay here in this trailer until we go home tonight. Then tomorrow, when we return to work on the house, you won't be able to run and play. You'll have to sit in the trailer again. If we can't trust you to obey us in the little things, like what is good for you to eat, then we can't trust you around all these tools and workers. Because you can't obey Mom and Dad, you'll have to stay in the trailer until you decide to tell us the truth about what you did today." I then prayed for him and asked God to lead him into all truth. I left him alone while I sat just out of sight on the steps of the trailer. At least an hour went by.

Finally, Zach peeked his head out of the door and said through sobs, "Mommy, I'm sorry. I took the candy. I lied. Please forgive me."

I thanked him, I told him I forgave him, and we prayed and hugged and went to get Daddy. "Daddy, I'm sorry. I took it. I lied. I'm sorry." His whole little body was shaking. The tears of repentance seemed like they were coming from his toes. It was dark, well past suppertime. We were all exhausted. Keeping Zach on the straight and narrow had taken hours out of our day. I bundled him up in my arms, and we all went to get dinner. Before we were a block away, he was sound asleep. His face shown like an angel. Peace once again reigned over his heart and mind. That was one of the last spankings we had to give him because we noticed that word pictures, stories, and separating him from the action had a greater impact than the pain of the spanking.

Because he was such a rough-and-tumble little boy, physical pain meant next to nothing to him. He could tough out any physical pain. But he loved to be part of the action, so time-outs were more effective.

However, when Zach was even younger, time-outs were not always easy to enforce and didn't work well with him. He was so strong willed he wouldn't stay where we put him. I had to literally stand and hold him into the tiny time-out chair. The more he struggled, the longer the time-out lasted. I had to choose well when to send him into a time-out because Zach's size and physical strength were exhausting me.

I found I had better results when I sat him on my lap in the rocker. "Zach, we have to take a time-out. You are out of control, and you could hurt yourself or your brother, so we're going to sit still in this rocker together until you calm down." Then I'd hold him close to me and rock back and forth. The more he struggled, the tighter I hugged him. I whispered in his ear, "Mommy loves you, and she wants what is best for you. You need to calm down and let your arms and legs rest. They have taken you into trouble, and we need them to not do that anymore. So let's sit together and rock, and I'll sing and pray. We'll ask God to help you calm down."

So we'd sit and rock, and I'd sing and pray in quiet whispers. Sometimes nearly an hour passed before he calmed down.

Zach had many of the signs of ADD or hyperactivity, but Bill and I wanted to see if we could calm him with diet, structure, and good parenting before we tried any medicine. We invested a lot of energy and creativity, but Zach did learn self-control. We found that if we wore him out physically each day, he was easier to parent. We made sure that Zach spent plenty of time each day playing outdoors. As soon as he was old enough, we had him in sports, where he not only tired himself out—he excelled. He began to feel great about himself. We also discovered humor worked well on him when he was just being rowdy but not defiant.

If he was just grumpy and out of sorts, I'd scoop him up and say, "Do we need to shake the ickies out of you? Are they hiding in your fingers" (then I'd jiggle his fingers), "or are they hiding in your toes?" (then I'd jiggle his toes). We'd make our way through each body part, and he'd giggle with glee. When I'd set him down, he'd be happy and obedient a little longer. I learned this trick from a mentor mom, a dear grandmother who had babysat Brock. She did it for me one day as we walked Brock to the car. He was not wanting to go, and it changed his mood so dramatically I decided to try it before I resorted to more drastic discipline measures.

Here's a checklist to consider before you discipline your child:

Is this my problem or my child's? Sometimes children are simply being inconvenient, not defiant. No child should be punished for a parent's mood swings. I received more compliance from my kids if I was honest with them. "Honey, I'm sorry we can't do that right now. Mommy has a really bad headache. Let me take my medicine, and let's lie on my bed. You can look at books, and I'll rest my eyes. Then maybe later this afternoon, when I'm feeling better, we can do that."

What is the simplest answer that will keep the boundary or rule in place? When our kids were young, simply giving them another toy or another game as a distraction often worked. Sometimes humor worked, like the "shake the ickies out" game or the "Rice Krispies" game. This game is great when you catch a child ready to break a rule but hasn't yet. I'd say, "Oh, no! It looks like Caleb needs an operation! He wants to do something wrong, but we can just take that desire out. Let's see, cut him open" (I'd pretend to cut him open by tickling him on his tummy in a straight line). "Okay, now let's pour in the Rice Krispies. Let's pour in the milk…Snap, crackle, pop…snap, crackle, pop!" I'd tickle his tummy as I said those words until he would squeal in delight. It would usually break the mood or train of thought so I could start him on another activity.

Can I reason with him? Helping children to listen to reason and turn their attention is always preferable. But young children often find reason to be an unwelcome guest in their world. Early in preschool, reasoning doesn't get their attention very well because they just can't understand abstractions like cause and effect.

Does she feel penned in? Can I offer choices and still get compliance? Giving children choices reduces the showdowns. I want my children to be dressed for school, but almost anything in their closet is okay. I want them to eat breakfast, so leftover pizza is just as valid as scrambled eggs. Sometimes children rebel because they feel like clones of their parents. Real discipline helps them be the best "them" God can make them.

Is this more of an issue of immaturity than defiance? If the problem was caused by immaturity, such as boredom because the rest of the group is older and can enjoy an activity but Mr. Two-Year-Old is bored and ruining everyone else's fun, simply choose an alternative. If the toddler has a tantrum over all the alternative options, give a time-out. I had a rule of thumb: If in doubt, give a time-out. If a child is truly being defiant, things will probably get worse. A time-out can stop the downward spiral.

Does this defiance or dangerous situation warrant a spanking? If it does, then do it privately, never in front of others. Explain the infraction fully, looking your children eye to eye and making sure they understand why they are being corrected.

Would natural consequences make a longer-lasting impact? Do you need to remove a privilege? What would happen if the child were older? Can you mirror a consequence that might happen later in life? Natural consequences can work very well. You might restrict a favorite activity:

no TV, no friends over, no going to friends. But don't just take away; add something: "Since you can't get along with your brother, there will be no TV tonight, and instead you may go clean your room." I learned a lot from my close relationship with my grandparents. The unruly teenage boys in the extended family spent a summer working on my grandfather's farm. If the boys snuck out and partied and drank the night away, Grandpa would just wake them up earlier and have more physically demanding chores for them to do. He'd say, "Just keep 'em tired and they won't have the energy to get in trouble." When our own children got older and wanted to bow out of a social responsibility or a family activity, we'd say, "Sure, you can stay home, but here's the list of things that need to be done by the time we get back." It was amazing how appealing the family activity became!

Years before we had kids, we heard Dr. James Dobson say the goal of discipline was to shape the will without breaking the spirit. Boundaries and structure help children turn their self-centeredness into God-centeredness and other-consciousness. A child who has been raised with consistent discipline and structure actually gains the most important tool for success—self-mastery. People who can and will do what is right regardless of their feelings have a head start over the rest of society.

If your children are old enough, involve them in a family forum on discipline and help them see why obeying Mom and Dad is so important. Give each child one or more of the verses below on discipline and ask them the same question: Why are you better off when you are disciplined?

- The fear of the LORD is the beginning of knowledge, but fools despise wisdom and discipline (Proverbs 1:7).
- For these commands are a lamp, this teaching is a light, and the corrections of discipline are the way to life (Proverbs 6:23).
- He who heeds discipline shows the way to life, but whoever ignores correction leads others astray (Proverbs 10:17).
- He who ignores discipline comes to poverty and shame, but whoever heeds correction is honored (Proverbs 13:18).
- Buy the truth and do not sell it; get wisdom, discipline and understanding (Proverbs 23:23).

Decision Point:

Be Consistent

Mom and Dad must be on the same page. Take an evening and talk about how you will both discipline. Train your kids first, and then when they willfully break the rules, some order of discipline is in order. Decide whether you will give a warning or require first-time obedience. Who will give the discipline? (We decided to rotate discipline and not do the "Wait till your father gets home" thing. We wanted Dad getting home to be a thing to look forward to, not a thing to dread. We decided the person who saw the infraction, disciplined the infraction, and since I was a stay-at-home mom, to even things out, when we were together, Bill handled things.) Decide on creative consequences, or at least decide you will talk behind closed doors and determine consequences instead of arguing in front of the kids. Write down your discipline guidelines for easy reference.

THREE

Decide Character Counts
How to Develop an Inner Compass

෧෧෧

I (Pam) sat in the rocker and held my beloved firstborn. He was just a few months old when we moved back to my hometown to become youth pastors in our home church. As I rocked back and forth, I thought of what the world might be like when my son would be a young adult. Things were rapidly going downhill in the culture. Drug use was on the rise. Suicide was the leading cause of death among teenagers, and alcohol-related deaths were a close second. We heard rumors of a new deadly disease that spread through sexual contact, while television and movie stars acted as if wrong were right. As a new mother, I was overwhelmed by the thought that my innocent son would have to someday grow up and face this world. If things continued, the world would be a very corrupt place, maybe even as dark and far from God as Sodom and Gomorrah had been. I shuddered at the thought.

Bill and I talked about these things often because he was serving as a youth pastor while our children were toddlers. Watching the downward slide of society, we knew only children with a strong inner moral compass would survive with their faith intact by 18. So we decided character counts and developed a plan to construct an inner moral compass.

Lord, Help!

As I prayed, God's Spirit reminded me that I was not the only mother to pray such a prayer. One such mom had a son during the time Pharaoh was killing all male Hebrew children. He feared the people he had enslaved would grow more numerous and stronger than his own people and would someday overthrow him. Jochebed could keep her son quiet by nursing as the soldiers spread through the streets, searching house to house, but soon he would be too big. His cries of hunger would be too loud to muffle with the milk from her breasts. What then? "What can I do to save my son?" she must have cried out to the Lord.

An ingenious plan unfolded in her mind. She would take a basket, a basket she had woven with her own hands, and cover it with pitch to make it waterproof. She would place the baby in it, lay it in the bulrushes of the river Nile, and pray no one would find him. She prepared for the day and instructed Moses' older sister, Miriam, to place the baby in the basket and follow it should it move down the river. The basket did drift, and Miriam must have prayed in panic as she saw it heading directly to the palace steps where the princess, Pharaoh's daughter, bathed. The princess directed her maidens to draw the basket from the river and was delighted to find a tiny baby inside.

Quickly thinking (and probably still praying), Miriam spoke out to the princess in a reverent whisper and arranged for a wet nurse for the baby. Miriam ran home, fetching her own mother to nurse her child in safety. As a wet nurse, Jochebed received protection and privilege. As Pharaoh's son, Moses had the best the world had to offer. Jochebed knew God had given her these precious years, brief but strategic, to prepare him to be a man of God within the palace walls. But what could a mother say? What could she teach? How much could she really impart in such a short amount of time?

My mind reeled as I thought about how Jochebed must have prayed, "God, give me wisdom. Give me discernment and clarity, to know what I should say, what I should sing, what I should pray, what I should teach, and how I should teach it."

Four Key Areas to Develop

I searched through tens of books to find out how long Moses and his mother were together. The commentators' guesses ranged from a few years to maybe five years.

I thought, "What would I teach, what would I sing and say and pray if I knew I'd only have five years to influence Brock?" Then I thought about the teens my husband and I worked with in ministry. "Lord, some kids seem to have what it takes to soar, while others stumble when they turn 18. What's the difference? What character traits, relationship and life skills, and spiritual skills do those who succeed have at 18 that give them the strength and courage to step out well into their calling?" I made a list of four key areas with these headings: Spiritual Skills, Relational Skills, Life Skills, and Character Qualities.

I began to brainstorm words and phrases under each heading. I tried to picture what priorities I'd have for Brock as he entered into the adult world. I knew he would learn some things after he left my influence, but I also realized he had to learn many things before he left home. I decided to focus first on the skills and character qualities he would need to have strongly in place before he was a teen.

Spiritual Skills

How to love God
How to pray
How to share his faith
How to prepare a Bible lesson
How to lead a discussion group
How to disciple another
How to walk in the power of the Holy Spirit
How to handle temptation
How to obey God

How to follow and lead
How to choose a church
How to discern his spiritual gift
How to develop a servant's attitude
How to learn basic doctrine, theology, and church history

Character Qualities

Honesty

Fortitude

Initiative

Neatness

Compassion

Empathy

Loyalty

Integrity

Courage

Contentment

Insightfulness

Resourcefulness

Flexibility

Creativity

Humility

Relational Skills

Conversational skills

Manners

Mediation

Delegation

Social graces

Respect for the opposite sex

Respect for authority

Respect for elders

Life Skills

How to take care of personal belongings
How to care for a home
How to care for a pet
How to care for a car
How to save money
How to interview for a job
How to earn more responsibility or advance in a career
How to balance a checkbook
How to be a lifelong learner
How to make appointments with medical and legal professionals
How to drive
How to use public transportation, travel, and tip

How to survive in an emergency or in the wilderness
How to use basic technology: radio, stereo, camera, computer
How to cook and clean

Photocopy the chart on the next page and list a few qualities and skills you want to focus on for each of your children this year.

Tools of the Trade

One of the most important ways to build these character traits in each of your children is by providing a well-rounded education. Your children are growing up in an intellectually driven information age. If they are to find their place, they must be well prepared with the basics of language, writing, reading, math, history, and critical thinking. To accomplish this goal, a parent must make many choices for a child.

Parents have three major choices for a child's education: public school, private school (secular or religious), and homeschool or independent learning. We have been in ministry for more than 20 years and have seen godly Christians use each of these choices to achieve the goal. We do not believe one choice is necessarily more spiritual than the others. Rather, each year, for each child, parents should reevaluate what schooling option is best for their child.

Instead of telling you *what* to choose, we will provide principles on *how* to choose which is best for your child. We have listed the benefits and drawbacks we have seen in each system of learning.

Child Care Choices

Let's start with child care decisions, which begin the moment a baby is born. Here are some facts to consider about that choice:

Children gain more confidence and security later in life if they have bonded to one primary infant caretaker.[1] So the question isn't "Do I work?" but rather, "How can I become a primary caretaker? How can I ensure a stable beginning and a secure bonding with this child I brought into this world?"

Toddlers and preschoolers need a safe environment, freedom to learn, and a small social circle. Selma Frailberg, while a professor at

By the Time You Are 18

Character Qualities

Relational Skills

Spiritual Skills

Life Skills

the University of Michigan, discovered that children under three fared best when cared for by mother. Those three to six years of age could sustain absence from mother for half a day but didn't do well with a prolonged absence of ten to twelve hours.[2] The question then becomes, how can I best meet these needs? And how do I decide when and if a child under five should have care other than parental care?

Are my motives for wanting to work outside the home centered on God? (Both Mom and Dad should ask this question of themselves.) We can easily fall into the trap of using jobs to fulfill needs *God* wants to meet in our lives—needs of acceptance, camaraderie, and interdependence. Or we may use our jobs to meet ego needs by providing financial success, a title, or the ability to order others around. Are you ready to sacrifice your child's interests to satisfy your own ego?

And yet, if your basic expenses exceed your income, you may legitimately need a second income. In those circumstances, how can you still choose what is best for your marriage and family?

In that case, first ask, *can we add a second income and still have one parent at home with the child?* Many at-home business opportunities are available today. Some marriages can survive tag-team parenting; some cannot. It is *not* in the best interest of the child if Mom and Dad are feeling estranged from each other and are tempted to get their emotional and physical needs met outside the marriage. It is *not* in the best interest of the child if a tag-team child care arrangement leads to a divorce. But it is also *not* in the best interest of the child for bills to go unpaid on a regular basis.

If a family-owned business, an entrepreneurial opportunity, or telecommuting don't work for you, then you must consider other child care options. Here are some questions to ask yourself:

Is a family member available for child care who would be a positive role model and who would love our children the way we do? Sometimes Grandma or Grandpa, a sibling, or an aunt or uncle would welcome a day or two a week with a child. We have been impressed with some amazing grandmothers. One set of grandmothers worked with the parents so that one grandmother comes Monday and stays through Tuesday. The other grandmother comes Wednesday and stays through Thursday. Mom then takes Friday off each week. The impressive part is that neither grandmother even lives in the same city as the grandchildren. They commute several hours each week to do this so that Mom, a pediatrician at a teaching hospital, can work into a practice that will allow her more flexibility someday.

Is a homelike environment available that comes with high credentials or high recommendations? This could mean care in your own home or in a home day care. The smaller the number of children cared for, the more like a family home setting it will be.

Some child care options truly do provide well for the social, educational, and emotional well-being of a preschooler. However, these are not easy to find. Consider the source of the recommendation, the enthusiasm of the other children, and the child care provider's willingness to invest in your children the way you would raise them. To have a successful experience, the provider must be willing to be a teammate with you, the parent.

Is my child ready for a more formal child care setting? Preschool options abound. When choosing a preschool, a parent needs to have many safety assurances: Is the building safe and clean? How long have the staff been employed? (Quick turnover is not a good sign.) What are the credentials of the teaching staff? Of the school itself? Can you contact other parents to get their opinions? Does the instructional style agree with your parenting style?

For example, Montessori preschools may be more open to child-led learning and taking advantage of teachable moments. Other preschools are more regimented and scheduled. Some provide many learning options like outdoor play, art, music, and spiritual education, while others provide only the basics of letters and numbers. The only way to know is to visit each school for a while and observe. Are they willing to provide part-time care according to your schedule? What is the cost? (The most expensive are not always the very best, but you often get what you pay for.)

Would you be seeking a preschool option even if child care weren't the issue? For example, parents of an only child or parents of children who were born many years apart will often seek out other children as playmates to enhance the development of social skills. Others want to make sure their child is ready for kindergarten, and they seek preschool hours for their child to accomplish that goal.

Each of our own sons was a part of preschool-like settings, but they were all different. Brock received wonderful preschool instruction once a week while I attended Bible Study Fellowship. Zach received great loving care two mornings a week after he was age four at a friend's home day care while I took a class to complete my education. Caleb, when he was four, attended a church-run preschool two mornings a week while I wrote. Each time, the major factor in the decision was our personal trust of the people who cared for our son.

School Daze

Now, here are some items to consider when you decide how to educate your school-age children.

Public School

Strengths

- Opportunity to be a part of the neighborhood
- Credentialed teachers with a graduate education
- Strict background checks for staff
- Opportunity to witness for Christ and influence others to come to faith in Christ
- May provide special services to developmentally challenged or excelling children
- May have extras like libraries, computer labs, and science labs
- Higher pay may attract better educators.
- Minimal additional cost because taxes fund the school
- Parents can work during school hours. Some schools might offer after-school activities for kids.

Weaknesses

- Cannot give any spiritual education and may even be hostile toward your child's expression of faith

- Secular accreditation that most likely includes teachings of beliefs that may oppose yours
- May devalue parental values or traditional family values
- May incorporate a tenure procedure that protects poor teachers
- May have larger class sizes, limiting personal attention
- May not value parental involvement
- Peer values and influence may not be what you would want reinforced.
- Budget expenditures may not be beneficial to your child.
- Children of faith can become disillusioned, discouraged, and even depressed by the sinful behaviors, attitudes, and actions of those around them.
- Classrooms may feel out of control (or actually be out of control) because the majority of students may not have been taught respect for authority and respect for others. Administration may not support teachers' classroom discipline policies.

Christian School
Strengths
- Bible-based curriculum
- Christian teachers and role models reinforce your beliefs.
- Usually smaller class size
- Usually more personalized educational plans
- High opportunity for parental involvement
- Respect for authority is encouraged.
- Security and confidence builds as children see parents, teachers, pastors, and faculty all modeling the Christian faith.
- Opportunity to come to faith in Christ as a result of school curriculum
- Opportunity for children to see parents sacrificing for higher priorities

- Positive peer interaction
- Parents can work during school hours, and some schools might also offer quality after-school programs for kids.
- For a single parent, teachers of the opposite gender can serve as role model in your child's life.

Weaknesses
- You pay tuition while your tax dollars support the public schools.
- Some have lower pay scales, so they may not attract top educators.
- Some may have strict background checks and high educational standards, while others do not.
- Students may develop an "us against the world" attitude or a fear of the real world.
- Some parents may abdicate their role as spiritual mentors.
- A few students may develop a "been there, know that" attitude at church because they have been exposed to Christian teaching all week at school.
- Some families might choose to work too hard to provide a Christian education, thus producing very limited family time because of two demanding careers.
- May not offer programs or staff for special-needs students

Private Non-Christian Schools

(Note: Private non-Christian schools will have some of the advantages and disadvantages of both public schools and private Christian schools.)

Strengths
- Smaller class sizes
- More personalized attention
- Parental involvement and quality control
- Opportunity to lead
- Opportunity to share Christ

- Tuition might provide more opportunities for arts, science, and technology.
- Stronger discipline and class order

Weaknesses
- Some faculty with opposing beliefs
- Some students may challenge your child's beliefs or values.
- Christian students might take flak for their faith or lack opportunity to express their faith.
- Tuition
- Some might lack perks of larger institution

Homeschool
Strengths
- Co-ops provide opportunities for personalized education in areas of specialties (music, science, art, technology, ministry).
- Very flexible on time, days, use of school hours, and learning methods
- Close interaction with adults produces fewer negative behaviors.
- Individualized pace
- Ultimate teacher-to-student ratio
- Flexible schedule allows for different models of learning (including traveling to the places you are learning about).
- Flexible schedule allows ample time for outside interests.
- Good for families that live in remote areas
- Students can explore areas of interest to them and not have to wait for the class or do busy work.

Weaknesses
- Not enough social interaction on the peer level if the parent isn't careful to involve student in other outside opportunities

- "Been there, know that" attitude at church because of Christian-based curriculum at home
- Expense of buying books, classroom supplies, and furnishings
- Home feels like school.
- May be more difficult for parents to both work outside the home
- May complete high school education very young and not be emotionally or socially ready for college

Questions to Ask When Considering School Choice

1. What are your top three priorities in choosing your child's education?
2. What are the lifestyle implications for each choice?
3. What areas of your child's overall development are you most concerned about?
4. What are your child's strengths? Which schooling option will reinforce those strengths and provide opportunities for future growth in those areas?
5. What are your child's weaknesses? What does each option offer to correct those weaknesses?

God loves your children even more than you do. As you prayerfully consider all your options, you can rest assured that He will lead you to make the right choices.

Decision Point:

Create Opportunities for Character Development

1. Create your own list of traits and skills you want to make sure to pass on to your children by the time they are 18.

2. Discuss possible child care options. How do they serve your priorities for child care, love and affirmation, safety, affordability, and education?

3. Create an education plan. Every child deserves a fresh evaluation and decision once a year.

A Graduation Prayer

(A letter written to Brock Farrel from your mother before you were a year old, to be read on your eighteenth birthday.)

I pray that by now you will have embraced and lived out your own faith in Jesus. I want you to have fallen in love with your Savior firsthand, not relying on Mom and Dad's faith but on a strong faith of your own. I want you to know the joy of walking moment by moment in the power of the Holy Spirit. I want you to be able to discern God's will for yourself.

I want you to have a rich prayer life. I want your communion with God to be personal and real. I want you to know how to use Scripture to pray, how to adore, confess to, and thank God, and how to supplicate on behalf of others and yourself. I want your prayers to be one-on-one worship experiences with the living God. I want you to really believe prayer works. I pray that by the time you are 18, you will have influenced others to believe God for big things and will have seen how a prayer movement can begin with just one—*you!* I want praise, music, and singing to come easily because your heart is rejoicing in the Lord's goodness. Sing—even if you can only make a joyful noise to the Lord!

I want you to enjoy great friendships. I desire for you the kind of true fellowship that can only happen when you choose to surround your heart with friends who love Jesus with all their hearts. I want you to have the courage and confidence to be a leader among your friends so they might draw nearer to Jesus because of you.

I want you to love God's Word. I want the Bible to daily be the lamp to your feet and a light to your path. I want you to know the thrill of walking in obedience to God—to find the gifts He's given you, to discern His will, to carve out your own ministry. I want you to have an eternal mind-set and a worldwide vision for what God wants to do. He'll do some of it through you! Regardless of your vocation, whether you are in full-time ministry or a secular career, living for Jesus is your first call. And if it is necessary to, I pray you'll have the courage of a Daniel or a Joseph and stand alone for your faith, your beliefs, and your convictions.

Someday you will meet that special someone—so we want you to then leave us, your mom and dad, and cling to the one God has sent you. Make your love life a priority when you marry, and you will always have the passion of life the world so desperately seeks after. However, if God calls you to a single life for an extended period, let your passion be set on living a pure life, and God will fulfill your desires.

Children are a blessing from the Lord. I pray you'll be a terrific parent as moment by moment you ask God for wisdom to tenaciously love and raise those who will bear your name.

I pray you will gain an education so you can enjoy the job God has for you. I pray you will save for the future, know the importance of tithing, and experience the benefits of being a self-motivated, hard worker. I pray you'll have a generous heart and share that which the Lord entrusts to you. I pray you'll be able to navigate the financial seas of credit, mortgages, checking accounts, and savings plans—all while being a good steward of all God has given. I pray you'll prepare well for the needs of your family in case of illness or death. I pray you will, above all else, keep a good name and good reputation.

I pray you will understand the huge price this country's forefathers paid and will be an involved citizen. My mother and my grandparents always reminded me that if I wasn't part of the solution, I was part of the problem. You know the solution to life's dilemmas—find a corner and make a difference! Be a leader. Be just and fair. Be a good friend and a fine neighbor. Treat others as God would treat you.

But please stop and smell the roses too. Let your heart be moved by a beautiful painting, a great piece of literature, or a moving drama. Take a few moments each day to see God's beauty around you. You are a part of that beauty. Your body is God's temple. Take good care of it.

Don't forget the little things. Say please and thank you. Eat right. Laugh. Keep your accommodation neat enough to find what you need when you need it or to minister to a friend at a moment's notice. Keep gas in your car and money in your wallet. Don't presume upon your guardian angel and go knowingly into danger unless another's life depends upon it. Now that you are 18, you are an adult and many others depend on you.

A time may come when my mind will fail and my body will refuse to cooperate with my will. At that time, I may depend on you. My prayer is that you will be there for God, your community, your church, yourself, your spouse, your children, your grandchildren, and the host of friends you will gather. And I pray that as you someday stand over my grave, you will rise up and call me blessed because I prepared you, with all God's compassionate help and wisdom, for this day. You are no longer only my child. Over the years together, you have become my friend.

FOUR

Decide to Have a Plan
Developing Kids to Be Learners and Leaders

಄಄಄

Faith is a treasure one generation passes to the next. But in the midst of a hectic life, how does one make space for passing the baton? Jill Briscoe, an international speaker and writer, passed her faith to her daughter, Judy. Judy once wrote to me about passing the baton:

> When I was about to become a parent, my mom said to always remember that no matter what I was doing—laundry, cleaning, cooking, or helping with homework—the ground between my own two feet was holy ground. In other words, I should be ready at every moment to use the opportunities God would give me to influence whomever He placed in my path for Him. This is something I remind myself about frequently. Some of the chores related to mothering can be mundane, yet if I approach all of these tasks with the expectation that He can use even the most basic chore in His plan, the chore isn't so mundane anymore.

I have three sons who are six, nine, and eleven. When my oldest son was almost four, he and my middle son and I were going to the grocery store. This was one of those mundane chores I didn't enjoy doing, especially because I had two little ones who would be asking for something in every aisle. As we drove to the store, my oldest son started asking some serious questions about heaven. By the time I pulled into the parking lot, he was saying that he wanted to invite Jesus into his heart. Before we got out of the car, Drew invited Jesus to be his Savior and Lord. This was a wonderful reminder to me that I needed to be ready and willing to use every opportunity to further His Word. The holy ground that day was the parking lot at the grocery store!

I too felt I was on holy ground as I thought about how to impart my faith to my children. I looked at a list of traits and skills I had written to remind me of what I wanted to build into my two preschool boys. I had instituted a quiet time where I read to the boys and then put them down on their beds in each of their rooms. I then turned on a Christian music tape and left them with Bible storybooks (hoping they would nap!). I told them each day, "Every day, God wants us to have a quiet time, a few moments to read and listen to God through His Word. Mommy is having her quiet time in the kitchen. Now it is time for you to have fun with Jesus. Just remember, you need to stay on your bed. The toys are resting, and God wants you to rest and spend time with Him. I'll see you in a few minutes." They usually made it through a book or two and perhaps one side of an audiotape before they drifted to dreamland. I held to my word too. I wanted to follow the example of Mary, Martha's sister. "Mary has chosen what is better, and it will not be taken away from her" (Luke 10:42). I tried to follow a pattern of delaying housework until after I had spent at least 20 minutes with God.

Discovering Key Traits

One day the list of traits I had written for my four-year-old was again on my heart. "God, I have that little chore chart on the refrigerator, but that is just teaching Brock personal responsibility. What about all those other traits? How can I know that I have a plan that will work all the traits into his life by the time he is 18? It seems as if there is more I should do." Then the Holy Spirit reminded me of a part of a talk I'd heard by Ken Poure when he was the director of Hume Lake Christian Conference Center. All I remembered him saying was that every year, on each of their children's birthdays, he and his wife took that child out and wrote up a yearly contract that included new privileges and responsibilities.

As I looked at my list of traits and skills, I felt a little overwhelmed. I knew I wanted Bill and me to be on the same parenting page, so I showed him the list and asked him to fill in anything he thought I might have missed. Then I shared my concern with Bill.

I wondered, "Which of these were really the most important? If we had to choose, which of these would we make certain happened?"

I (Bill) looked at the list again and began to group the items. I told Pam, "Honey, I think there are three main areas that these things on the list fall into: being a learner, being a leader, and loving God."

Love God. The various character traits are more likely to develop if a person is connected to Jesus. After all, the fruit of the Spirit is love, joy, peace, patience, kindness, goodness, faithfulness, gentleness, and self-control—that was almost half the list of character qualities right there!

Be a lifelong learner. Kids who love learning are motivated to acquire the practical and relational skills they need.

Be a leader. What about the rest of the list? What's the common thread? Most leaders have these traits. Confident people are those who are on the offense, taking back ground, not on the defense, huddled in a corner. I was raised to be a difference-maker. I want my children to be difference-makers too. But what if they are shy? What if they don't like the limelight?

As I (Pam) considered this, God reminded me of the study of women of the Bible I had just completed. Those women (Deborah, Ruth, and Esther) earned influence in a variety of ways. Some built a platform of influence through quiet service. Yes, they were leaders, but they used their own personality and leadership style. So I decided we'd focus on *loving God, being a learner,* and *being a leader.*

Implementing the Traits

When Brock woke up from his nap, I tried it out on him. "Brock, you know what I want you to be when you grow up?"

"A policeman?"

"You can be anything you want—a policeman, a pilot, a pastor like Dad, or the president of the United States. But regardless of the job you do, I want three things for you. I want you to be *loving God* with all your heart, soul, mind, and strength; I want you to always keep *learning* no matter how old you get; and I want you to be *leading*. I want you to lead your friends and not be a follower only. You can lead them using the talents, gifts, and strengths God will give you because there are all kinds of leaders. Brock, isn't it cool that they all start with an—"

"*L!*" he shouted.

"That's right, an *L*. Loving God, learning, and leading!"

All that day, as Bill and I saw these traits in Brock or his brother, we would comment on them and give the boys praise. We noticed Brock helping Zach pick up toys. "Brock, you are being such a leader! The best leaders are servants and helpers."

"Zach, you are looking at books. Books help us learn new things. You are a learner."

"Brock, will you bless our snack?" And after his short prayer, "Thanks for loving God. God loves hearing us pray to Him."

We were so excited. We felt as though we finally had a simple enough framework to weave positive traits into our children in a natural, daily, moment-by-moment way. But we kept thinking about Ken Poure's tradition with his kids on their birthdays. Brock would be starting school the following fall. Couldn't we begin some back-to-school tradition? I (Pam) write goals for myself each August, and Bill does the same each January. Why couldn't we do this for and with our children each year?

We prayed over the idea for a while. Then one day I created a little chart with some pictures cut out from magazines that showed various chores. Brock couldn't read yet, but the pictures showed things I wanted him to take responsibility for: brushing his teeth, making his bed, making lunch, feeding the fish. At the top I wrote "Brock is a learner and leader who loves God." I listed all the character traits on the back of the chart, and on the front I wrote one to focus on that first year.

Then I thought, "Yuck. This just seems like work to me. What fun is a chart? If all I do is lay out work for my kids year after year, what do they have to look forward to? At least Ken Poure took his kids out for lunch!

"Let's connect this to a special day! A Learner and Leader Day! We could do a fun family activity: bowling, movie, parks, maybe even Disneyland if we could ever afford it! Or maybe back-to-school shopping!

"That's it! Every kid loves Christmas and birthdays because of the presents. We'll give presents on Learner and Leader Day. Something to help them either love God, learn, or lead! Or better yet, something that does all that and applauds the uniqueness and calling we see God layering into their lives! Yes—a celebration of God making them leaders!"

When Bill got home from work, I could barely contain my excitement. I was hoping he'd be as excited as I was.

He was genuinely enthusiastic. "Honey, I think we should make it like a contract so the kids learn how business is run. And those relationship and driving contracts seem to be helping some families of kids in the youth group."

I quickly drew up a rough draft. "We could title it, 'Brock Is a Learner and Leader Who Loves God.' We'll list responsibilities on one side and privileges on the other. The leadership trait we are focusing on for this year will go on the top along with a verse for the year. He can memorize that verse to help him learn that trait. We'll choose it for now, but as soon as he is able, he can choose his own. I want our kids to take ownership of this process as soon as possible, and this seems like an easy place to start. Then we'll put the unique gifts God is giving each of them in a space at the bottom, and we'll add the date and lines for signatures, like our mortgage! What do you think?"

"Sounds good so far," Bill said, smiling. "As they get older, I think the kids should decide what consequences they should get if they break the contract. By the time they are in junior high, they should be owning their own life and their own mistakes, and we can be their coaches and biggest fans."

From this conversation came our first draft of the Learner and Leader contract, which is included below:

_____ Is a Learner
and a Leader Who Loves God!

Privileges:

_____

_____

_____

Responsibilities:

_____

_____

_____

Leadership trait to focus on this year: _____

Key Verse for the Year: _____

Unique Treasure We See God Unfolding in You: _____

Consequences:

    Violation 1: _____

    Violation 2: _____

    Violation 3: _____

Student's signature _____

Parent's signature _____

Date: _____

Then I added, "What if, when we present the gift, we do it with some kind of a blessing? You know, like in the Old Testament when Isaac blessed each of his sons. He had an awesome way of just speaking the truth over them."

"Definitely. We'll have to scale it back and make all this pretty simple while the boys are young, but I think this is definitely a plan that can grow with them."

The First Learner and Leader Day

The August before Brock started kindergarten, our finances were very tight. We had moved to San Diego and still lived in an apartment, and Bill had actually taken a pay cut to take a senior pastor position. Not many churches were looking for 29-year-old senior pastors!

I had about $20 to work with. I bought a lunch box and Thermos for $3.99. Brock loved McDonald's Playland, so we could take him to lunch there, and he could play. I bought him a new T-shirt and a pair of pants on sale for a total of $9. If Bill and I had Happy Meals too, we could give the toys to Brock, and he'd think he'd struck gold. I made up the Learner and Leader chart, wrote a verse with a permanent marker on the side of the lunch box, and added, "Brock is a Learner and Leader! Brock Loves God!"

We asked a friend to watch Zach so we could have one-on-one time with Brock, and we headed out the door to McDonald's. I explained the Learner and Leader tradition to Brock and then said, "Your dad and I have a gift for you. Each year we will give you a special gift to celebrate what God is doing in your life. Daddy has a special prayer he wants to pray over you first, and then we'll give you the present."

Bill prayed, "Dear God, thank You for our firstborn son, Brock. He is getting so grown-up that he's headed off for kindergarten tomorrow. Thank You that Brock has a strong sense of righteousness. He wants people to follow the rules, and he speaks up and reminds people to do what is right. Bless him this year as he seeks to do what is right and follow a new set of rules that will come with starting school. Amen."

Then I handed Brock the wrapped lunch box. As he unwrapped it, he could see an astronaut on the side of the box. "Brock, you are going into unknown territory just like an astronaut. In one of Dad's sermons, he told the story of some astronauts who did what was right. They were brave, and God brought them through.

"We see that same bravery in you. Last year, you spoke up and told someone that smoking would kill them. Last year, you made the junior high boy go down the slide the right way instead of climbing up the wrong way. You show your little brother how to do things right, and sometimes you even remind Mom and Dad of the rules. We pray you will always have bravery, integrity, and righteousness, and that you will always want to speak up for what is right. This lunch box is our way of saying, 'Way to go!'"

Brock beamed. Bill and I looked at each other and smiled. We knew this Learner and Leader Day tradition was a keeper!

Creating a Plan for Your Own Learner and Leader Day

You can decide to do a Learner and Leader Day at any time that works best for your family. For example, you might like to connect it with your New Year's celebration, when everyone is making resolutions. Or you might spread them out over the year, having one on each child's birthday (this option might be easier on the budget). You could have your Learner and Leader day in September to start the school year right. One woman I met at a Time Out for Moms conference has a virtue of the month, and she focuses her entire family on one character trait for that month. Every family is different, so you can adapt each Learner and Leader celebration to fit your family.

In our family we've also initiated a Summer Celebration, a kind of mini Learner and Leader Day. My children are on a traditional school schedule with summers off, so I want to make good use of all that free time. For our Summer Celebration we all buy new bathing suits, restock our beach bag with pool and beach toys, sunscreen, and new beach towels, and then I lay out special summer goals for each son.

For example, one year I wanted the boys to understand how the Bible came to them from the Greek and Hebrew languages. (We have a tradition that when each child can read John 3:16 for himself, he can choose his own new Bible.) I wanted the learning to be more hands-on and less from a book, so we made scrolls and hid them. When I gave them the go-ahead, our boys set out to find them. Then I told the story of how a shepherd boy found the Dead Sea Scrolls in some caves. We also studied how they were translated so meticulously. We read about the lives of some of the great leaders who had been martyred for trying to translate the Bible into the common-man's language and for printing Bibles so every person could have them. We read the biographies of men like Tyndale and Wycliffe. We studied the Reformation and Luther and nailed our own treatise to the garage door.

One fun day, while studying the history of the Bible, I told the boys about the Dark Ages, when even priests didn't have Bibles and many church leaders couldn't even name the 12 disciples. I told them it was a dark time in church history because of pagan beliefs and human hunger for power. The truths found in the Bible were hidden away because so few people could read, let alone read a Bible. I explained that this then led to some ugly acts in church history, like the Crusades, where men in the name of Christ massacred and conquered to gain wealth and power for the Church. And I showed them pictures of the tools of the Inquisition and explained how men and women were often tortured and killed for trying to get Bibles to families like ours.

Because so much of this happened in the Dark Ages, one day we made armor, swords, and shields out of newspaper for each son. This led me to a passage in Psalms where God says He is our shield (Psalm 84:11). We looked up Bible-time shields and found that they were as tall as a man, covered with metal and leather, and decorated. They were three-sided, so the only way a man could be hurt in battle was to step out from behind the shield or to turn and run in retreat. The boys caught on to this word picture quickly.

"Mom, that means that if God is our shield, we'll only get hurt if we run away from Him."

"That's right."

"Or if we step out from behind the shield—like disobey, so we're out of His will."

"Right again. Everything that comes to us in life must first go through God and His loving character before it gets to us. That's why we are told to put on the armor of God in Ephesians. God's Word instructs us so we know how to stay behind God's shield of protection."

"That's why you want us to have a quiet time every day?"

"Right again."

We spent many days that summer reliving days from the Dark Ages. We read Arthurian legends. We read the biographies of Christian reformers. We studied castles and knights. We watched movies with medieval themes. Then, at the end of the summer, we went to a medieval dinner theater where we ate food with no utensils and saw tools of the Inquisition and real knightly armor. The boys were amazed as they witnessed a reenactment of a knightly jousting competition.

That summer, I wanted my sons to come away valuing the Bible, but they gained much more. They gained a full appreciation of what honor meant. They discovered the horrible results that happen when God's Word is diluted, and they were introduced to the ongoing battle between good and evil. They even enjoyed acting out excerpted scenes from Chaucer and Shakespeare!

Choosing a Learner and Leader Gift

We have a set of criteria in choosing the gift:

It must be *practical*—something we might have to buy anyway.

It must be *personal*. The child should be able to tell we thought about the gift.

It must be *prophetic*, displaying the truth about the uniqueness, the calling, or the strength we see God building into each child.

Summers can be a terrific time to reinforce the values you want to develop in your child. If your kids go to school from September to June, use the summer months for these more time-consuming projects. Here are some ideas to spark your own thinking:

Look back. Buy a set of books that describe what children are supposed to learn in each grade. Your public school office should have a "scope and sequence" available to parents. Most private schools, or the publisher of the curriculum they use, should have something similar. Look over what they learned the past year and fill in the gaps with fun, hands-on learning projects. Often these can be integrated into plans for the summer vacation.

Look ahead. Scan what is coming in the next year or two in their education and visit places, rent movies, read books, and give gifts that would expose them to that field of learning. They will feel great about themselves when the teacher gets to this place in the curriculum. You don't want to teach exactly the same material, or your kids might be bored in class, but you can expose them to the subject. For example, if my child will be making a solar system in school, I might take the family to an observatory. Or I might buy a telescope and do some stargazing or get those glow-in-the-dark star sets and let them build their own solar system on their ceiling so they can appreciate it every night at bedtime.

Look deeper. Apprenticeships and internships were once the norm for preparing for productivity in the adult world. You can create opportunities for your children to be exposed to areas they might be interested in. Call professionals in that field and ask if you and your child might shadow them for a day. If the child is an older, responsible teen, you wouldn't need to go, but you don't want to give the appearance that the professional would be babysitting. Offer to help the pro succeed. Be a part of a road crew, offer to work a day for free, or help him with a special event or major project. Encourage your children to go to the people at the top if they want to be at the top when they are older. Set up some adventures that will help shape your children's future.

Look for adventure. Have your children brainstorm the first day of summer vacation all the wildest places, people, and things they'd like to go, meet, and try. Then prioritize the list and plan in Fabulous Fridays—a reward adventure for working hard all week. Feel free to add your ideas to the mix. Many cities have parenting magazines that list all kinds of learning adventures from drama and computer camps to visiting a llama ranch or the opera!

Look for enterprise. When my children have time off from school, they always want to go, do, and spend! I look for ways to help them earn their own money to spend on their own interests. Mark, a man in our church, set up his son, Jesse, with his own plant business that runs just two weeks before Christmas. They go to a nursery and get whatever plants Jesse thinks will sell (a lot of poinsettias, of course). Then Dad and son travel to all the businesses in the community to sell their wares. They spend their earnings on Christmas gifts. Some families use the holiday season for craft shows, others use summers for lawn mowing or lemonade sales. I spent my summers on 4-H projects from raising livestock to home decorating. I got to keep my ribbon money from the fair to buy something I wanted to learn more about. Also, my animals were sold, and that money helped me get through college.

Look for the issue. Summers and school breaks are great times for special testing for learning problems, special tutoring, or a second pass through that algebra class that didn't go so well during the year. One summer, I had two of my sons tested because certain subjects just seemed to be very difficult for them. The learning specialist laid out a personalized plan. Your local public school is obligated by law to do testing, but you can find other professionals at learning centers, through college educational programs, or through professionals in the education field.

Look for the possibility. Summer is also a great time for inventory tests that will help your tweens and teens decide what their assets, strengths, and talents are. Crown Christian Financial has an online Career Pathways inventory that tests a person's personality, values, work setting likes, skills, strengths, and weaknesses to then give a personalized list of recommended professions. We also had two of our sons take an inventory that assessed strengths and weaknesses and gave a list of recommended careers based on raw IQ and basic intellectual assets. SOI (Structure of Intellect) Systems gave them a list of careers they would excel in based on eight basic standards like their ability to handle figurative issues, symbolism, semantics, comprehension, memory, evaluation, problem solving, and creativity. One of our sons discovered that engineering, art, and design were his top scoring fields, which was great information as he entered high school and had to set his course plan.

We set a plan to use school breaks and summer vacations to enhance his art and design education.

You don't have to call your celebration day Learner and Leader Day. You can make up your own name, like "Back to School Bonanza" or "Goal-Setting Getaway" or the "Smith Summer Send-Off." The only things you really need are the components of a Learner and Leader Day: (1) responsibilities for the coming year, (2) new privileges, (3) a leadership trait to focus on, and (4) a gift and blessing to applaud God's strength and calling in a child's life.

Praying for the Traits

Choosing the leadership trait to focus on for the upcoming year is probably one of the most important components of the Learner and Leader principle. Each year, Bill and I pray most of the summer and ask God to show us an area of weakness or incomplete character aspect in each of our sons.

For example, we have one son who was very, very shy. He wouldn't even ask for ketchup at a fast-food restaurant. Most of the time we had to order for him because the clerk couldn't hear him. He would regularly ask his brothers, "Tell them…" or "Can you go ask for me?" We knew we had to help him find his spine! One year we chose *initiative* as his trait, and we applauded him anytime we saw him do anything on his own. He received a standing ovation from our family the first day he went back to the counter and asked for ketchup!

Another of our sons was pretty rough around the edges. He was a real jock and not very verbal. He made noises rather than words to get what he wanted. He was capable of more grunts, groans, and squeals than the average boy. On top of that, he thought bodily functions, and the noises they made, were entertainment. He burped regularly at the dinner table, used his sleeve and underside of his T-shirt as a napkin, and wiped his nose on his T-shirt shoulder or one of his brothers' shirts just to hear them scream. I remember thinking, "This kid will never get married! He's going to live with me the rest of his grunting and burping life!" That year we chose *being a gentleman* as his leadership trait. I taught him manners, or shall I say, *re*taught him over and over again. We used our china, crystal, and linen napkins more that year than any before or since. We often ate by candlelight because he liked to light the candles and would sit more quietly at a table lit by candlelight.

That year, when the science fair rolled around, we brainstormed ideas of what the kids could do their projects on. Zach, my rough-around-the-edges gentleman-in-training said, "Mom, I know you hate it when I burp. What if I do a project about what makes me burp?"

"I'm all for this idea, but I'm not sure how you'd run a scientific test to show how and why people burp. Let's go to the library and see what's there."

When we went to the library, I ran across an experiment book that showed how to measure the amount of gas in a soda. I showed it to Zach.

"Cool. I can use this to test different kinds of soda to see how much gas they have. Mom, I promise I will never again drink the soda that has the most gas!"

So we ran a test using different sodas in baby bottles and balloons. He discovered that the darker the soda, the more gas it contained. As a result, cola was out! Zach was so proud of that experiment. He won the first-place ribbon and a science set for his class. And when the winner for the entire school was announced—it was Zach!

In my mind, I remember sighing with relief and thinking, "Maybe there's hope."

A few weeks later, a friend called me to report what had just happened at a birthday party she had given for her daughter. Seems Brock and Zach had sat down to eat pizza when Zach looked around and noticed that there weren't enough spaces for the moms at the party to sit down.

He elbowed his older brother in the ribs and said, "We should get up and give the moms our seats. That's what a gentleman would do." My friend didn't take the seat but ran to the phone to call me and left a message, "You'd be so proud of Zach! I think he will get married someday after all!"

Passing the Traits

One of our favorite families is my sister-in-law's. We have been friends with her parents, Bill and Janeen Ezell, and then with Erin, since before she married my (Pam's) brother. We have seen firsthand how well they live out their faith. Janeen is known as one of the best Bible communicators in her region. Erin is one of the best drama producers and directors in any church in the country (maybe we are a bit biased!). They are effectively passing their love for ministry to the next generation as our nieces are now carrying on the tradition of creatively sharing the message of the faith, as you can tell from the following comments by Janeen, Erin, and Erin's then-13-year-old daughter, Rebekah.

As a child, even one raised in a non-Christian home, I (Janeen) somehow believed that Jesus was God. It wasn't until I was grown with two children of my own that I came to learn about the person and position within the Godhead called the Holy Spirit…that He connects us with God in a personal way and also guides, counsels, comforts, and teaches us everything about Jesus and His will for our lives. When my children accepted Christ at an early age, I expected and taught my children that they would have the very same Holy Spirit living in them…not a miniature or child-size version, but the very same Spirit that filled Paul, Peter, and every believer. I expected that if they asked God in prayer, they would receive and experience the very same guidance, wisdom, and comfort as myself—I expected, and God did not disappoint them or me.

For as long as I (Erin) can remember, the only thing I ever wanted to do was be a great mom, just like my mom. She was energetic, smart, beautiful, and fun. She loved God and knew Him unlike anyone else I ever met. I thought that the greatest thing I could ever be was to be like her. Even in high school, as my friends were pursuing college and careers, I prayed for a Christian man to love me and allow me to be his wife and a mother. I attended college and entered a career with a major oil company, but my hopes remained the same. When I was 20 years old, my dreams became a reality. I met and married a wonderful Christian man who loved me, and four years later I became a mom.

Now, as the mother of three children, I understand more deeply the incredible woman God gave to me as my mother. The courage she demonstrated in trusting God for me and my brother was so apparent when I became a parent myself and sent my precious child off to school for the first time. Her devotion is still so remarkable to me. I now sit by my children when a fever or flu ravages their little bodies, and I remember the many times Mom was there for me. Her understanding of God's Word and the time she took to study, read, and pray challenge me today as I struggle to fit all my responsibilities into each 24 hours. The greatest blessing of my life has been to have a mother who loved me, who cared for me, and who diligently taught me the joy of knowing and understanding God's Word. It is my greatest inheritance. My highest aspiration is still to be just like my mom.

The thing I (Rebekah) have seen in my Nana is the ability to communicate God's Word to other people so they can comprehend it and understand the promises God has for us. I also see that she is a loving, caring, and compassionate mother and Nana. These are the qualities I admire in her, and I hope that she will always stay that way.

What I see in my mom is a great, God-given talent. She can take music, scripts, sound, and lights and make them all into a presentation of God's Word. Through her direction, we can tell the story of Jesus' birth, life, death, and resurrection. I also admire her perseverance and imagination. She is loving and caring too.

Because of them, I do not want to be a person that is all show and no tell. I want to have depth. I want to be able to communicate God's promises to everybody. I want to be able to present them in an imaginative and creative way. I also believe that God will change me and mold me to have the amazing attributes of my mother and Nana.

These three women demonstrate how God can lead, guide, and carry faith from one generation to another, then another, then another. How will you choose to pass the baton to your children?

Decision Point

Build Responsibility into Your Children

Sometimes passing the baton means you need some creative options to motivate and move kids into action. Read the ideas below and the list of what kids can handle at what ages and create a plan to move your children into action so they can learn to be responsible adults by being responsible children.

Magnet motivator. One mom writes, "In our home, each morning I place my children's responsibility magnets on the left side of the refrigerator. When they wake, each child checks his or her magnets to see what they need to do before they can leave for school or go out to play. As they complete each task, they move the corresponding magnet to the right side of the refrigerator. The magnets are easy to make. For the nonreader, pictures, symbols, or simple drawings can give direction. If the child makes his or her own set of magnets, they experience a higher level of ownership and are more highly motivated to move the magnets."

Help them bloom. Write responsibilities on Popsicle sticks and each day have each child choose one or more. This is great for routine tasks, such as setting the table, clearing dishes, and washing dishes. One mom made flowers to go on top of each Popsicle stick. A vase of paper flowers sits atop her dining room table as a daily reminder to keep the kids involved.

Work for hire. Pay an allowance (we chose $1 per week for each year of a child's age) as a reward for assigned work (starting at age 5). Here's the catch—they pay all their own "fun" expenses. To make the arrangement more businesslike, if you have to clean up after them or do their chores, charge them a housekeeping fee. Family Tools, Inc. offers a unique chore chart. Educator Cheryl Eliason created PEGS (Practical Encouragement and Guidance System), which is a flexible, versatile organizational tool that will get your kids off the sofa and in action (www.familytools.com).

The big payoff. When my sons were small, I motivated them by moving marbles from the sad jar to the happy jar anytime they did anything that would make Mom, Dad, or God glad. A certain number of marbles earned a special treat after dinner—usually a special activity with Mom or Dad. Sometimes the treat was tied to bedtime, like a flashlight to read under the covers. Another version of this is Super Kid Tickets. Give your kids tickets for positive reinforcement and allow them to save up tickets and redeem them just as they would at an amusement park. Rewards like these can stretch out children's attention spans and raise their goals to bigger rewards. They learn delayed gratification, a trait that will help them soar through their teen years!

Review the highlights. One mom I know, Tammy, sings a song about the highlights of each of her children's days while scratching their backs. Michele asks her children questions to get them talking at the end of the day: "What did you do to make God smile today?" For ideas, get *Mom's Jar of Questions.*[1]

Make a game of it. I used games to motivate my boys, as does Maria, who sets a timer and makes cleaning up a race! She makes mealtime fun by having each child pretend to be a person at a restaurant. One person is the waiter, another the hostess, and so on.

Date with Mom or date with Dad. All children, regardless of their age, love a parent's undivided attention. The key to making this a strategic motivator is to let the children choose what to do on the date. Have a budget that is enough to get their attention. If you are working on a big attitude or behavior change, the carrot needs to be big enough to keep them trying.

Freeze. When motivating kids to work out a sibling rivalry, try freeze tag. When kids are in conflict, my friend Tracy yells "Freeze!" and all the kids have to stop exactly where they are. No one can move until the conflict is resolved. Joy brings everyone to the table, and everyone shares what the issue is and what they would like to see happen to solve the issue. No one can eat till the issue is resolved! If Karen hears a negative comment, she stops the accuser and extracts two compliments for every put-down she heard.

Life report cards. Lynn says, "My mom always said, 'Give people bouquets while they can enjoy them.'" One mom of a son with a learning disability gives a Life Report Card when the school report cards come out. She gives him As in areas he is strong in: kindness, Lego building, and sharing. Esther has created a more God-centered reward system. Her children each have a points chart where they earn points not only for good grades and completing chores but also for expressing positive character qualities like respect, good manners, and sympathy.

Good morning! Jenny greets her children with this little song: "Good morning, God, this is Your day. I am Your child, teach me Your way." Use birthday mornings to build esteem. Shawn climbs under the covers with her birthday child and retells the story of his or her birth and her delight to have such a wonderful gift from God. My own mom woke us up on our sixteenth birthday with breakfast in bed at the hour we were born.

Reward growth with opportunities for growth. Nancy, whose son is now a divinity professor at Harvard, rewarded her children's Bible memorization with family "mystery trips" to the zoo, a bookstore, or other fun learning site. She went out of her way to reward excellence with opportunities to learn in an excellent setting: Christian camps, mission trips, and teaching younger students. It is no wonder that when her son attended Wheaton College and was looking for a mentor, he walked into the president's office and asked the president himself—who said yes!

You can do it! Jaime's little girl was anxious about being left for the Sunday school hour, so her mom began to tell her, "I know you are going to have a wonderful time. I know you are not going to cry. I know you are going to be a good girl and that the teacher will tell me super things about what a good helper you will be." By telling her daughter the positives beforehand, her daughter began to look forward to Sunday school. Jodie homeschooled her son until he was 11. On the eve before he was to attend "real" school, as he called it, he was a little nervous. Jodie wrote down a few Scripture passages about God's presence and strength and tucked them into her son's shirt pocket. The next day, anytime he was anxious, he pulled out a card and read it. Years later, as a 21-year-old college student, he is still in the habit of tucking God's Word into his heart—not just his pocket.[2]

More Than You Might Think!

What Kids Can Do at Various Ages

Ages 2–4

Pray

Retrieve things you need

Put away toys and books

Set table

Clear own plate (use plastic ware)

Brush teeth

Wash hands

Ages 4–5

Put away groceries

Set and clear table

Put clean silverware away

Make bed

Dust

Fold towels

Get own snacks (make a snack drawer they can reach)

Get own cereal, donuts

Make simple sandwiches

Pick up room (mark and label with pictures to make it easier)

Ages 5–6

Help plan meals, help at grocery stores putting things in the cart

Begin cooking (microwave and simple baking from a children's cookbook)

Separate laundry, mate socks, put away clothes

Answer phone

Help with larger chores like washing car

Help with planting or raking in the yard

Carry in groceries

Ages 6–7

Lay out clothes for school

Water plants

Handle own bath

Write simple thank-you cards

Cook easy meals

Hang up clothes

Rake, recycle, compost, take out trash

Bring in wood for fireplace

Clean bathroom

Empty dishwasher

Get ready for bed

Get mail

Call a friend

Walk to next-door neighbor's house

Take care of own bikes, skates, and balls

Take care of simple pets (fish, cats, gerbils)

Ages 7–9

Neighborhood errands (in a cul-de-sac or on same side of the street)

Short errands when accompanied by older friends or older siblings

Sweep walks, hose patios

Vacuum house and car

Responsible for own lunch money, homework, sports equipment, and hobby pieces

Mop floors

Iron with supervision

Help with younger siblings

Tithe

Fold clothes

Almost any household chore if trained and supervised

Begin quiet time with Jesus

Strip and remake bed

Learn to sew and mend

Clean blinds

Help with campfire, barbecue

Paint with supervision

Organize closets, own room, drawers

Go places and return at specific times (get your child a watch)

Help in ministry (greeter, help with younger children, pass out flyers)

Ages 10–11

Clean refrigerator

Learn how to use washer, dryer, dishwasher

Wait on guests

Be responsible for own hygiene

Plan parties

Junior High

Local errands on bike (in safe neighborhood)

Responsible for own appointments, own calendar

Stay alone and babysit

Decorate room

Learn adult crafts

Social etiquette and boy/girl relations

High School

At the high school level, teens are adults in training. As they enter high school, plan out how you will systematically give them control of their lives. For detailed advice, see *Got Teens?* by Jill Savage and Pam Farrel (Harvest House).

FIVE

Decide to Be Creative
Developing a Map to the Hidden Treasure

∾∾∾

Humility is a virtue. John Wilmot, the Earl of Rochester, once said, "Before I was married I had three theories about raising children. Now I have three children and no theories." Author Phil Callaway sums up the way many parents feel with the title of his book *I Used to Have Answers, Now I Have Kids.*

Most families include at least one child who is a challenge. If God blesses you with more than one child, you are virtually guaranteed that at least one of them will be obstinate or stubborn or demanding. Parents who used to be idealistic commonly find themselves at the end of their rope—at a loss for what to do and what to say. Some of you know this feeling intimately. You've lost your patience, you've lost your way, and you might feel as if you've lost your mind. We're convinced God sends strong-willed treasures to us so we don't become self-sufficient or fall into the trap of thinking we are the perfect parents. God wants to remind us that He is the only one who has all the answers!

Our strong-willed treasure is son number two, Zachery Johnathan Farrel. We should have caught on about the time he started walking.

We were at a church afterglow (that delightful event where 500 men, women, and children crowd into a church fellowship hall to eat cookies and drink red punch). Zach was playing quietly with toys at my (Pam's) feet, pretending to be a compliant child. I was engaged in some deep girl talk when suddenly one of the students from the youth group came running up to me.

"Pam, do you know where Zachery is?"

I looked down at the floor. He was not there. I looked around, scanning the feet of the crowd. Then I began to panic, but the teenager said, "He's over there, eating someone's Bible."

I ran across the gym, shooting up a prayer. "Lord, let it be someone who can handle it!"

None of this should have surprised me. Because Zach put everything in his mouth, I had poison control on speed dial.

I spotted him in a corner, blissfully gnawing on the corner of a beautiful new black Bible. I picked him up, pulled the piece of Bible out of his mouth, and tucked it in my pocket. Then I looked to see whose Bible he had eaten for dinner.

Fortunately, it belonged to our associate pastor. Whew! I ran across the gym to find him.

"Doug, I'm so, so sorry. Zach, he...um, he ate a page from your Bible."

Good-hearted Doug just laughed and in his sweet Southern drawl said, "Augh, just watch. It's probably 1 Corinthians 13, and I'm just gonna have to love your kid!"

I pulled the crumpled piece of Bible out, and sure enough, 1 Corinthians 13 was on one side of the page.

Before each of our sons was born, Bill and I chose his name and created a plaque with its meaning and a verse that captured that meaning. This is Zach's:

Zachery

The Lord Has Remembered
JEREMIAH 15:15-16 NASB

Thou who knowest, O LORD, remember me, take notice of me, and take vengeance for me on my persecutors. Do not, in view of Thy patience, take me away; know that for Thy sake I endure reproach. *Thy words were found and I ate them,* and Thy words became for me a joy and the delight of my heart; for I have been called by Thy name, O LORD God of hosts [emphasis added].

Zach had already lived up to his name verse!

The Beginning of the Treasure Hunt

When Zach was barely able to walk, he ran. And he ran everywhere. At the park one day while I was unloading Brock from his toddler seat, Zach unhooked himself from his seat, opened the car door, ran straight for a 30-foot sculpture in the center of the park plaza, and shimmied straight to the top before I could even catch up to him.

When Zach was about 18 months old, he put me on alert about what a challenge he might be to raise. I put him down for a nap but soon heard some noise coming out of his room. When I went in, I found he had climbed out of his crib, done some kind of superman leap, grabbed the three hanging baskets, and swung himself over to his changing table. He had dumped everything out of the baskets and was now emptying two bottles of baby powder all over the room. It appeared to be snowing in the nursery!

I carried my powder-white son to my bed and said to him, "Zach you stay on this bed! I will be right back."

As I cleaned up the mess, I went back to my room to check on Zach, who was, of course, *not* on the bed where I had told him to stay. Instead, he was in my bathroom, where he had broken all the childproof locks on the cabinets. He had stuck an assortment of my sanitary pads to his body, and he had tampons sticking out of his nose, his diaper, and his ears. He looked up and proudly said, "Look mom! Stickers!"

When we began building our house in San Marcos, Brock was a little over five, and Zach a little over three. Zach and Brock both received little carpenter's belts and plastic tool sets, but Zach was always replacing his plastic toys with the real things. He actually was a very good helper. He would hold one end of the siding up and hammer in nails as well as many adults who came to help. Zach loved a challenge.

One day I (Bill) was working on the framing of the house while Pam had an errand to run. Brock and Zach wanted to stay and play on our new property, and I promised to look after them. Before I knew it, Zach had climbed up a 30-foot eucalyptus tree (these trees are fast growing, straight, and very flexible. To a kid it would be like climbing a ticking metronome). Zach delivered his famous line: "Hey, look at me!" I looked to see my son up in the tree, higher than our two-story home. Zach had his arms and legs wrapped around the thin tree trunk, and he was making the tree sway back and forth. I knew if I panicked, Zach could let go and fall three stories to the ground. But if I did nothing, Zach could get that tree swaying so much it would break in two, and he would come hurtling down. So I coolly said, "Yeah, uh-huh...that's good, Zach. Can you come help Daddy?" while I frantically begged God to bring him down safely. Much to my relief, our little monkey simply shimmied back down the tree.

We've always said Zach marches to the beat of a different...accordion. He was exceptionally agile, always landing like a cat on his feet. But he was also exceptionally nonverbal. He preferred making noises instead of forming words or sentences. And he was strong-willed! He and the youth pastor's son stole change out of the offering one Sunday when they were not quite four. They were headed to the church school kitchen to buy snacks when we caught them.

The Spiral Down

When Zach was almost nine, he had a medical problem that he couldn't control that added to his daily frustration with life. He had an older brother who threw up if he ever lied, so he rarely did anything wrong. In fact, Brock got most of his rebellion out of his system before he was two, and it's been pretty much easy sailing with him. When our youngest son, Caleb, came along, Zach, who had previously been the darling baby, was bumped from his prima donna position in the family to that dreaded middle spot. Bill and I were sensitive to his plight, so we were careful to never compare the boys.

We committed ourselves to applaud Zach's unique strengths. Zach was a talented athlete. He taught himself how to ride a bike at age three when he found Brock's in the driveway. Zach simply jumped on it and rode away—first time, no wobbling, no falls, total confidence. He did that with rollerblading—down a hill the first time out on skates. He was also a courageous skateboarder and mountain biker. *No Fear* T-shirts were made for boys like our Zach.

And Zach was a good-looking kid. People often commented on his handsome appearance and his strong, fit body. His eyes danced and sparkled at the thought of a new adventure or challenge.

But when he was almost nine, life seemed to be sapping his tenacity. He began to lose ground in school. Homework each night became a battle. He only made progress when we placed an M&M at the end of each row of math problems.

He became more and more sullen. He acted out with more and more explosive anger at his brothers. He hated anything new. Any change in the routine or plan sent him reeling into a tantrum. Our brave, happy-go-lucky, adventurous son was turning inward, spiraling downward into a depression, drowning in a pain he was unable to articulate. We fought to keep his head above these emotionally turbulent waters.

One day he came into the house from playing outside with his brothers. Brock and Caleb were in tears. He was beating on them again. Zach stomped into the house, bumped one brother and socked the other right in front of me.

"Zach," I bent down and whispered intently into his face, "you cannot do this. Hitting is inappropriate. Go upstairs, and I will come up to talk to you."

Zach stomped up the stairs, knocking his brothers over in the process. He slammed the door to his room and threw a baseball at it, knocking a hole in the door. He then picked up his favorite clay art piece he had made and smashed it into the wall, breaking it into little pieces. I bounded up the stairs just behind him. I prayed all the way up the stairs because I had made a commitment to never, ever discipline in anger. But I wasn't angry. I was scared for my son.

I walked into the room, bent down so I was eye to eye with him, and said firmly but calmly, in more of an intense whisper than a yell,

"Zachery, this is inappropriate. I know you are angry. I know you are upset. But you cannot use your fists to show it. You have got to learn to use words to express your feelings."

Zach exploded and yelled back at me, hands on his hips, "You want words! You want words! Then I hate myself and I hate my life and if God made me, I hate Him too!"

I listened in shocked silence. Then I simply replied in a whisper, "I'll be right back."

I ran to my room in tears. I threw myself across my bed and desperately prayed to God, "Lord, I'm a pastor's wife who is raising a little atheist upstairs. I am so afraid for Zachery. I don't know what to do. I know he is angry at his medical condition. He might even be upset because it has made him gain some weight so he might not feel like himself. Maybe being in the middle is hard. I don't know. I don't know anything anymore. All I do know is that Psalm 139 says he is fearfully and wonderfully made. I believe You placed a gift in each and every one of us. But God, Zach is so angry he cannot see the treasure You have placed inside him. Help me help him see that treasure!"

Making a Treasure Map

Then the idea came. I ran to the office and pulled out a piece of poster board. I drew a treasure map on it with a collection of lines and a treasure chest at one end. I glued two quarters onto the map and marched back upstairs where Zach stood, just as I had left him.

"Zach, here's the deal. You and I are going to go on an adventure. See, God has placed a treasure, a special uniqueness inside every person. There is a treasure in you, Zach," I said as I tapped on his chest. "You and I and God are going on a treasure hunt to discover that hidden treasure. So here's the plan. I am going to ask you every day to name one positive thing about your day and one thing you think you did well. Then once a week, while everyone else is in second service at church, you and I are going on a breakfast date, and we're going to talk about what we see God is showing you about the treasure inside you. We're going to do this for at least six weeks, maybe eight. At the end of that time, I'm going to invest some money. I'm going to invest that money in the treasure God has shown is in you. Zach, you are a special guy. We all love you, and God loves you most of all. Let's ask God to help us discover your treasure."

I prayed over him, and then I asked him to pray. All that came out through his sobs and tears was a faint, "Help me, God."

The next day after school, I got the treasure map down off the wall where I'd posted it. "Zach, what's one positive thing that happened today? Let's write it down."

Zach looked at his feet silently. "Come on, honey. Just one positive thing about your day." He kept staring at the ground as if a hand would appear and write the answer on the carpet in front of him. This response, actually a nonresponsive attitude, had become familiar to me when dealing with him. I felt that the drawbridge was up and alligators were in the moat. Zach had a chronic Eeyore-like attitude. Eeyore, in the Winnie-the-Pooh tales, always hung his head, moped, and said, "It's hopeless, it's never going to work." That was Zach—hopeless.

I spoke for him, "Honey, you are alive." I was holding back my own frustration because I was sarcastically thinking, "Yep, you are alive— because I haven't killed you from sheer frustration, kid!" But God miraculously replaced my frustration with compassion, and I wrapped my arms around that sullen, stiff little body and whispered excitedly into Zach's ear, "Zach, you're alive! You're alive. I am so glad God gave you to me! You're Mama's special treasure!" And I took the pen and wrote on the poster: "Zach is alive."

The next day, right after school, Zach ran upstairs and brought the treasure map to me. He had several answers to the two questions.

Soon, there weren't enough lines to hold all the positive things Zach was seeing around him. Each week, he couldn't wait for our mom-son date. And every week, I learned more and more about him. Because he still struggled with finding the words to express himself, I took out a magnet that had faces that expressed different emotions. The magnet had a little square on it that said, "Today I feel," and Zach could move it to faces that express emotions: exhausted, confused, ecstatic, guilty, suspicious, angry, hysterical, overwhelmed, frightened, and a host of others ranging from excited to depressed. I taught Zach the meaning of each word, sometimes acting out how the feeling looks and how people act if they are feeling that way. I read and read and read everything I could find about children and their feelings. I adapted every learning activity I had ever heard about or used in any setting to try to teach Zach how to understand and express verbally what was going on inside his head.

Sometimes he became frustrated because he couldn't find the words to use to help me understand him. At those moments, often as he was screaming or thrashing about in anger, I would simply wrap my arms around him and hold him ever so tightly, and whisper, "I love you, Zach. Nothing can make me not love you. You can never push me away. I'm here to stay. You and I and God will figure this out. Nothing's too tough for God. Nothing's so tough that my love and God's wisdom can't handle it. I'm here, baby. I'm here. I'm here." I found that when I reacted with stubborn love, he felt securer and safer. He eventually was able to think better, and slowly, he would try a new way of expressing himself.

Week after week, I was tapping into the real Zach—the Zach God had created. Zach and I were beginning to see his treasure.

At the end of those eight weeks, I had discovered a lot about my son. I had always known he loved sports, particularly biking and baseball. What I hadn't realized was that Zach loved those things because he loved the camaraderie of the experience. I knew Zach had many friends (which actually stumped Bill and me because we wondered how a kid who didn't speak much at all could make friends). Zach loved people. People gave him energy. Being with people motivated him. We began to see a pattern. Zach was often stubborn because he feared new things. We discovered we could always convince him to try something new if we appealed to his sense of loyalty to a person. The people who expressed to Zach how much he meant to them personally were the ones who got the most out of him.

We also discovered he loved music. And we saw another repeating pattern on the map. Zach loved to set and reach goals. We learned so much about our son in just two months' time by following our treasure map. It was fun and exciting for all of us.

With the money I had set aside, I bought some baseball equipment. I bought some tickets to a Christian concert for Zach and some of his buddies. We filled in the treasure map from Christmastime until about Zach's birthday at the end of February. Then baseball season started.

Zach made the all-star team. At the end of the season, the coach brought Zach up in front of his teammates and all the parents while he said about my strong-willed treasure… "Zach has the best attitude of any kid I have ever coached."

I wanted to joyfully proclaim, "You don't know how far he's come! Praise God!"

Dad's the Difference

While Pam was helping Zach discover the treasure inside, I (Bill) was teaming up to convince Zach God's plan was best. When Zach was in his Eeyore mood, sitting and declaring for the umpteenth time, "I can't do this. I'm so stupid," I sat with him until his attitude started to turn.

We have seen in more than 20 years of ministry that the stronger the child's will is, the stronger Dad needs to be. When we say Dad is stronger, we don't mean more physically aggressive or verbally abusive—far from it. Rather, Dad needs to be tenaciously diligent to speak the truth in love, back up every discipline plan, and not cave in.

For example, when Zach would say "I'm stupid," and refuse to do his homework, I would simply say, "You are not stupid. Do not say you are stupid. Zach, you can have a good attitude or a bad attitude, but either way, you are doing this." Or I might say, "You can make this hard on yourself or easy on yourself, but you are doing this." Once when one of Zach's pouting tirades had extended for hours, I quietly but firmly told Zach, "Son, I will outlast you."

It is amazing what can happen when Dad and Mom form a united team, backing each other up, relieving one another when they become frustrated, and finally outlasting the strong-willed child. (Suggestion to single parents: The single moms in our church who handle their children best have banded together to have a support net so that if they are exhausted and need backup, they can call one another.)

The earlier a child knows that Dad means business and will always keep his word, the better for the strong-willed child. These kids are looking for boundaries, and they want to know they can depend on you. They respect commitment even when they don't like it. To keep this message in front of Zach, I invested time in Zach with father-son trips, coaching his basketball teams, and helping him with special school projects.

Pam and I often prayed together for and with Zach, that God would lead him out of the quicksand of negativity and onto the solid ground of the truth. I was tenacious in reminding Zach, "We will never force you to be like your older brother. We don't expect that and neither does God. We want you to be Zach. Just be the best Zach you can be."

I spent hours building skateboard ramps with Zach, taking him to skate stores and competitions, and scanning photos of him skateboarding so he could create posters, clothing decals, and other high-tech identity icons. I recognized that skateboarding was one way for Zach to do something excellent in an area Brock wasn't good in. Fortunately, all these efforts had an impact. His grades improved, and so did his attitude.

But strong willed means the struggle is continuous (with short breaks to regain your parenting strength!). The summer before he entered high school, our athletically talented son announced he didn't want to go out for football, even though he had spent the past two years talking about playing the sport. He'd already decided that even though he was a baseball all-star, he didn't want to play baseball next season. We had him in gymnastics because he was excellent, but when his friends moved he wanted to quit. We made him complete the year because Farrels finish what they begin, but every trip to the gym was stressful for all of us.

"I don't want to do football. That's Brock's thing," he said.

I (Bill) replied, "So you're telling me you don't want to do it because Brock is good at it?"

"Yep."

"But you're good at football also."

"So?"

"Zach, I cannot let you make decisions this way. I love you too much. If you don't want to play football because you want to do something else, that's fine. But you cannot live in reaction to Brock."

"Everybody will compare me to Brock, and I hate that."

"Zach, you're different from Brock. You're stronger than he was at your age. You're faster than he was at your age. He is an offensive player, and you will probably be a defensive player. Just be you, Zach. You and God decide what you are good at and then go for it."

"I don't know, Dad. I just don't want to be like my brother."

I looked Zach in the eyes and with firm determination said, "This kind of thinking is going to be bad for you. I will be all over you until you decide to make the decisions that are right for you. I will follow you around school if I have to. I will bug you every day if I have to. Whatever it takes, I will do because I love you too much. Please do not think I am kidding about this, Zach. I am committed to helping you find yourself."

Channeling Zach's hyperactivity and strong will was exhausting work. But when you are battling for the life of your child, no sacrifice is too high.

Fast-Forward

During Zach's senior year, we were in Dallas for a national coed cheerleading competition. We were riding an elevator with a mom and her hyperactive young son. The elevator was crowed, so the little boy was like a ball in a pinball machine. He was pinging from person to person and bumping into everyone. I looked over to spot his exhausted mom leaning against the side of the elevator, trying to ignore her rowdy son's behavior. Finally, after he almost knocked a couple people down, she couldn't ignore it anymore, so she barked out, "Zachery!"

I bent down to face the lad. "Zachery! I have a Zachery. He was just like you! He had a club called Hyper for God, and only little boys like you can join. He found he could learn to use his hyperactivity for good. He went from Ds in junior high to a 4.0 in high school. He was third string on his freshman football team until he decided to use that hyperactivity to train. He has now played first string on varsity for three years. We are going to watch Zach. His cheer team is first in the nation, and the University of Louisville has offered him a scholarship for college. Would you like to meet him?"

He didn't answer, but his worn-out mom did: "I want to see him. I want to see a miracle!"

If you are in need of a parenting miracle, ask God into the center of the issue and trust His creativity to replace your frustration and fears.

Going the Distance

First Kings tells the story of a woman who was willing to take a risk on behalf of her son. Elijah was a prophet of God, and God had a plan for providing for Elijah's need and for the widow and her son, but they didn't know it yet. This is what God said to Elijah:

> "Go at once to Zarephath of Sidon and stay there. I have commanded a widow in that place to supply you with food." So he went to Zarephath. When he came to the town gate, a widow was there gathering sticks. He called to her and asked, "Would you bring me a little water in a jar so I may have a drink?" As she was going to get it, he called, "And bring me, please, a piece of bread."
>
> "As surely as the LORD your God lives," she replied, "I don't have any bread—only a handful of flour in a jar and a little oil in a jug. I am gathering a few sticks to take home and make a meal for myself and my son, that we may eat it—and die."
>
> Elijah said to her, "Don't be afraid. Go home and do as you have said. But first make a small cake of bread for me from what you have and bring it to me, and then make something for yourself and your son. For this is what the LORD, the God of Israel, says: 'The jar of flour will not be used up and the jug of oil will not run dry until the day the LORD gives rain on the land.'"
>
> She went away and did as Elijah had told her. So there was food every day for Elijah and for the woman and her family. For the jar of flour was not used up and the jug of oil did not run dry, in keeping with the word of the LORD spoken by Elijah (1 Kings 17:9-16).

Look Back

What has God already done for you? He gave you this child. He gave you His Word, which explains that God created this child. He knows every hair on his or her head. He has provided to keep you and your child alive. God even gives encouraging reminders in His Word: "With man this is impossible, but with God all things are possible" (Matthew 19:26). "Nothing is impossible with God" (Luke 1:37). God can do "exceeding abundantly beyond all that we ask or think" (Ephesians 3:20 NASB). Look back, thank God for your child, and thank Him for every provision or bit of wisdom He has already given. As you look back, your faith will be built up for the future.

I (Pam) keep quiet-time journals and prayer notebooks where I record my requests. When times get tough with my children, I read those journals and notebooks. I also pull out our photo albums. Sometimes seeing reminders of God's faithfulness in the past gives me the faith to step forward and deal with the present.

Get the Best Help Possible

When a tough time comes for your child, don't waste time worrying—go directly to the top. Go to God and ask Him for a solution. Go to the best Christian leaders in the field. Go to the best doctors. Now is not the time to worry about hurting someone's feelings. When a child is drowning, you don't take an opinion poll on the beach to see who the crowd feels is the best rescuer. Instead you run to get the lifeguard, a person trained to rescue—an expert.

That's what the widow did:

> Some time later the son of the woman who owned the house became ill. He grew worse and worse, and finally stopped breathing. She said to Elijah, "What do you have against me, man of God? Did you come to remind me of my sin and kill my son?"
>
> "Give me your son," Elijah replied. He took him from her arms, carried him to the upper room where he was staying, and laid him on his bed. Then he cried out to the LORD, "O LORD my God, have you brought tragedy also

upon this widow I am staying with, by causing her son to die?" Then he stretched himself out on the boy three times and cried to the LORD, "O LORD my God, let this boy's life return to him!"

The LORD heard Elijah's cry, and the boy's life returned to him, and he lived. Elijah picked up the child and carried him down from the room into the house. He gave him to his mother and said, "Look, your son is alive!" (1 Kings 17:17-23).

We believe parents should take this principle of going to the best one step further: Get the best advice and training *before* you need it. When I (Pam) was still single, I went to the Campus Crusade for Christ Institute of Biblical Studies. At age 19 I sat for weeks and listened to Dennis Rainey, now the president of *FamilyLife Today*, talk about marriage and family. When Bill and I were newlyweds, we watched all of the James Dobson videos on family even though we didn't have children yet. When we were expecting, we worked through *Preparing for Parenthood*, a Bible study by Norm Wright. We also found another Bible study entitled *Discipline Them, Love Them* extremely helpful as we prepared to be parents.

When Brock was less than a year old, I listened to *Focus on the Family* radio daily. I also added programs like *FamilyLife Today, Parent Talk, The Family Workshop, Crown Financial Concepts,* and other family programming. I have subscribed to all kinds of parenting magazines, and before Brock was a year old, I had read more than 100 books on parenting. I figure if I get one good idea from a book, it's worth the money I paid for it.

When Brock and Zach were just toddlers, I hung out with several older women who were leaders in Bible Study Fellowship, and I watched how they parented. I asked Nora, a woman who had four terrific kids, two in our youth group and two in full-time Christian service, to be my mentor and share with me how she parented. I had a wonderful mother, but I came to Christ before my mom, and we grew in Jesus together. My parents also had a turbulent marriage because of my dad's alcoholism. They were not able to model for me a mom and dad who both loved God and loved each other during my developmental years. I gleaned from my own mother all the wonderful, creative ways she mothered me, and I know my tenacious love comes from her example, but I wanted more information for my own family.

I also made careful observation of the families in the youth group we pastored. I watched the parents of the best kids in the youth group, and I even started a list in one of my quiet-time journals called, "Things I will never do when I have teenagers: Hills _not_ to die on."

On that list were things like these:

- Do not freak out if my 15-year-old daughter wants her own phone. If she wants to pay for it, let her.
- Do not ground my kids from youth group. Find another way to punish them, preferably working them hard and limiting TV, social activities, and other things not related to God.
- Care less about the length of their hair and more about the condition of their heart.
- Do not make my kids be a certain way just to make me look good.
- Do not live through my children. Have my own life, have my own dreams and goals, and let them have their own dreams too. My dream for them may not be their dream. Be more concerned that they find God's dream for their life, not one I might have for them.
- Do not be legalistic. Major on the majors.

With these thoughts swimming around in my head, when Zach hit his tough spot, I knew God would have an answer. I knew to pray and plan, and not to react out of fear, frustration, or anger. I had a host of positive reinforcement ideas already in my head, and I had example after example from real life and from the Bible of what tough love and committed love looked like. By preparing and informing yourself ahead of time, you are less likely to make a mistake that will make matters worse.

Patient Parenting Produces a Prize

Today, I have a new son. Zach's nickname around our church when he was in high school was "Pastor to Preschoolers" because he worked in children's ministry. He knew the name and personality of every kid in the department. They followed him like the Pied Piper around church. Zach excelled in skateboarding, and he tried his hand at guitar lessons because music provided one more way for him to express himself. However, by far, Zach's strength is in helping people. He is a sensitive motivator and a great friend. He is the most attuned to my emotions. He'll often notice if I have a headache or if I seem preoccupied or stressed. He has a fun sense of humor, and he loves to make people laugh.

As a freshman in a public high school, Zach went out for football. He started out third string, a far cry from his older brother, the starting varsity quarterback. But being the star isn't what is important to Zach. People are.

During his freshman year in high school, Zach held a pizza party for his teammates at which he shared his personal testimony, including a piece of his story: "Guys, God gives me the strength every day to face my fears. Right now, God is giving me the courage to talk to you. God can give you that same strength and courage if you ask Him." That day 16 of his teammates prayed to receive Christ. His coach has affectionately nicknamed him The Preacher because of his positive impact on the team. At the freshman football dinner, his friends saved him a spot and wouldn't start eating until Zach came in and selected someone to pray over the meal.

While reading one of his college freshman English papers, I learned he was the one teammate a female cheerleader called after she had taken an overdose of sleeping pills. Zach rushed her to the hospital and saved her life. Another time, he stood down an older student who had hit his girlfriend. Soon the girl moved out, freed from domestic violence. Recently, a friend was angry at his mother and hung up on her. Zach took his phone and called his mom back and said, "Hi, Mrs. Thompson. This is Tom's friend Zach, and he has something he needs to say to you."

Then Zach held out the phone and said, "Tell your mom you're sorry. You never hang up on your mother."

His friend apologized, and then Zach took the phone back and said, "As long as he is my friend, he will never hang up on you again."

People call Zach, and he has answers for their issues. Recently, I complimented Zach on his people-helping skills and said, "You might consider a career in counseling. Then at least you'd be paid to help all the people you help!"

"I've been thinking the same thing." It appears Zach is beginning to own the treasure inside.

Because he feels great about who God made him, he is able to make others feel great too. I spoke at a Time Out for Moms conference, and I asked my sons to make a video, giving advice to moms. This is what Zach said: "There was a time when I felt stuck in my life. I didn't like myself much, and I felt like a failure. But my mom never gave up hope in me. My advice is to never give up on your kid, no matter how hard it gets. My parents never gave up. My mom helped me realize I had a treasure, and that God made me special for His purpose. Your kid has a treasure too. Don't give up...go on a treasure hunt instead."

Decision Point
Be Creative

When dealing with high-need children, strong-willed sons and daughters, or those with learning disabilities or emotional issues, you will need to gather as many tools and skills as possible. If one method doesn't work, you need access to others that may be more effective.

You may have to become best friends with learning specialists, counselors, and educators. As the parent of a strong-willed, high-need child, you are your child's advocate. He may become the child other kids won't (or are not allowed to) play with, he may struggle with self-image issues, or he may create classroom disipline disruptions. Don't be discouraged. Stay the course. Stay in the game and battle for your child.

As parents, look at all your children and decide whether you need to hunt down some creative options. Decide whether you need to...

- make a doctor appointment
- make a counseling appointment
- buy a book to learn more
- purchase resources to motivate your child
- attend a parenting conference
- pray for a new idea, a new contact, a new friend who has been there

SIX

Decide to Be a Student of Your Child
Mapping Out the Uniqueness of Your Child

ονονον

When archaeologists are looking for treasures from past civilizations, they stake out an area, mark off plots, meticulously number them, and record every bit of information they find. They painstakingly chip, chisel, whisk, and sweep bits of earth away. These scientists are masters of observation. They know the smallest clues, when pieced together, can lead to the greatest finds.

In the same way, as we use resources to unearth clues that lie beneath the surface of our child's soul, we can be more effective parents by adapting to meet our child's needs. We can also guide more confidently when we draw on the wisdom available to us through specialists. We will share many resources that have helped us see our own children more clearly—the positive and the negative! Each resource we share contains a wealth of information. Since we will give only a snapshot, a bite-size piece of these helpful tools, we encourage you to buy each of these books and resources. As you make further investigation using each resource, you can piece together a beautiful mosaic of each of your children.

Understanding the Gender Difference

In our book for married couples *Men Are Like Waffles—Women Are Like Spaghetti,* we explore the differences in the genders. We devote an entire chapter to parenting boys and girls. In a nutshell, men are like waffles—they process life in boxes. If you look at a waffle, you see a collection of boxes separated by walls. The boxes are all separate from each other and make convenient holding places. That is typically how a man processes life. His thinking is divided up into boxes that each have room for only one issue. The first issue of life goes in the first box, the second goes in the second box, and so on. The typical man spends time in one box at a time. Social scientists call this "compartmentalizing"— that is, putting life and responsibilities into different compartments. Because of this kind of thinking, men are by nature problem solvers.

Women are like spaghetti. In contrast to men's wafflelike approach, women process life more like a plate of spaghetti. If you look at a plate of spaghetti, you notice that the individual noodles all touch one another. If you attempted to follow one noodle around the plate, you would intersect a lot of other noodles, and you might even switch to another noodle seamlessly. That is how women face life. Every thought and issue is connected to every other thought and issue in some way. Life is much more of a process for women than it is for men. This is why women are typically better at multitasking.

Parents should keep a few principles in mind for each gender. For example boys are the people of the ladder, and girls are the people of the circle. This means that one-upmanship is a necessary and expected behavior in a boy. He wants to be the best at something, and he'll risk interpersonal conflict to reach the top. By helping a son achieve and feel confident in an area, you will also help him become a better sport when he does experience loss. Keep in mind that a boy will strategically organize his life in boxes and then spend most of his time in the boxes he can succeed in. Boys can become too singular in focus, ignoring areas in which they feel less competent, so parents are wise to work extra hard to help their sons experience successes in areas that are vital for life, such as reading and math.

When men perform as well as they expect to, they tend to attribute their success to their own skill or intelligence. If they perform below their expectations, they tend to blame it on bad luck or some factor that is out of their control.[1] Parents can curb this habit of blaming others by teaching their son to own up to failure and take responsibility for mistakes.

On the other hand, women tend to underestimate their abilities, and when they perform only to the level of their low expectations, they tend to attribute it to their lack of ability or intelligence. But when a girl exceeds her low prediction for achievement, she tends to attribute it to good luck or some other factor beyond her control.[2] A wise parent will compliment her when she recognizes that her own hard work paid off. Women tend to lead by consensus, which can be a great people skill, but it could also hold them back if they have to take a vote on every issue that needs a decision!

Because our sons are like waffles and tackle one problem at a time, we have learned not to give a verbal to-do list: "Go get your black sweats, put your shoes away, take out the trash, and feed the dog." Rather, we write out the list (a piece of paper is a great "box"). Following lists will help young men learn to multitask.

When stress hits, boys will want to go to their favorite and easiest boxes (places where they feel successful or can unplug), and daughters will want to talk! Sons will feel more loved if they are given space to fish, to be on the computer, or do a hobby. A daughter will feel loved if someone listens.

Understanding Varying Personalities

Many great personality tools are available to help you identify the primary motivator of each personality type. Let's start with some basics. The chart on page 105 contains four quadrants, each with a unique personality. The personality types on the left are primarily people-driven personalities. I am married to one. Bill is a pastor, but he has a difficult time staying on task. Not because he can't. He graduated from seminary with honors. He was an architect major when I met him—but he didn't stay on track to be an architect. As he shared Christ and saw people's lives change, he knew he wanted to invest his life in people, not buildings. If he is working on a task and a person walks by who seems to be a little blue, Bill cannot ignore them to complete the task. People are his priority. That's what makes him a great shepherd—but it is also what sometimes keeps him from completing tasks efficiently.

Zach has this same trait. If he has a choice between breaking down the set after church or babysitting the staff kids, he'll entertain the kids in a heartbeat. If he has homework and friends come over, he has learned that he has to create a homework club so he can get his homework done. He studies best over conversation and chips. Brock, on the other hand, would rather lock himself away in his own room to study because he says, "Studying in a group is a waste of time. You have to wait until everyone gets it, and half the time they aren't even talking about anything remotely related!"

You guessed it, Brock is task-oriented. The task-oriented personalities are the two on the right side of the chart. Task-oriented people do like socializing, but if they have to choose between getting the job done and talking, they'll get the job done every time. When I wanted something done at home, I'd ask Brock, and he'd have it done in an instant so he could go on to the tasks he enjoys most. Many people who are great with technology have this personality trait. Brock can do almost anything on the computer I need done. He can fix VCRs and set up sound systems. He can build a set of bookshelves or a desk without even looking at the directions. He loves math. Life to Brock is one big equation. You put in the right variables, and you'll get the desired outcome every time.

But if you want counseling, don't ask Brock. His answer will always be the same. "You are having a problem with temptation. Don't give in anymore. Problem solved." If a person wants sympathy, Zach is a much better counselor. He'll sit down with a person, usually instigating the conversation because he can read discouragement or depression in a person's face. He'll ask, "What's wrong?" He'll listen attentively, he'll pray, and he'll carry their pain with him. He always wants to take people places and buy them resources he thinks will help.

Introverts and Extroverts

The personality types on the top are extroverts. Those on the bottom are introverts. Be careful. This doesn't necessarily mean one

PEOPLE ORIENTED	TASK ORIENTED

PERSONALITY TYPE I
POPULAR
Sanguine

Motivated by:
ATTENTION

Brawner: Otter
Phillips: Expressive
DISC: Inspirational
Littauer: Yellow like the sun
Biblical Example: John the Baptist

PERSONALITY TYPE II
POWERFUL
Choleric

Motivated by:
Being in CONTROL

Brawner: Lion
Phillips: Driver
DISC: Dominant
Littauer: Red like fire
Biblical Example: Peter

EXTROVERT

PERSONALITY TYPE III
PEACEFUL
Phlegmatic

Motivated by:
RESPECT & ACCEPTANCE

Brawner: Retriever
Phillips: Amiable
DISC: Steady
Littauer: Green like grass
Biblical Example: Barnabas

PERSONALITY TYPE IV
PERFECT
Melancholy

Motivated by:
ANSWERS & STRUCTURE

Brawner: Beaver
Phillips: Analytical
DISC: Cautious
Littauer: Blue like the ocean
Biblical Example: Martha

INTROVERT

is loud and the other quiet. Extroverts process life from the outside in while introverts process life from the inside out. As a result, extroverts feel more secure and at peace when all the ducks of their life are lined up. They tend to ask questions like these: "Am I spending enough time with God? Am I balanced in my personal disciplines of prayer, Bible study, witnessing, fasting, and memorization? Am I spending enough time with my family? Am I spending enough time with my friends? Am I spending enough time at work to meet the goals I have set?" They are life organizers, and if they feel they have the right organizational plan, they are happy as clams.

Introverts tend to ask questions like these: "Do I feel connected to God? Is my personal prayer life deep, and am I sensitive to God's call and leading? Am I sensing a connection with those I love? Am I relating well to my friends? Is my work fulfilling? Do I have a sense of personal peace and tranquility?" When these people are emotionally connected and fulfilled, they are at peace.

There can be quiet extroverts. Zach is an extrovert. For years we couldn't figure out how someone who doesn't seem to talk could have so many friends! Bill is an outgoing, verbal introvert. He is a gifted communicator who is entertaining and practical. At the same time, he has an ability to go straight to the heart, which comes because the heart is a priority to him. Bill is miserable if he is not emotionally connected to those he cares about.

The Four Basic Temperaments

We'll look at the ancient Greek names for the four temperaments and a few basic traits for each one: the original personality types: sanguine, choleric, melancholic, and phlegmatic. In her book *Raising Christians—Not Just Children,* Florence Littauer uses some terms that are much easier to remember:

- Sanguines are *popular.* Their personality is *yellow* like the sun.
- Cholerics are *powerful.* Their personality is *red* like fire.
- Melancholy people strive to be *perfect.* Their personality is *blue* like the ocean.

- Phlegmatics are *peaceful.* Their personality is *green* like grass.[3]

When taking a personality test as an adult, try to think back to what you were like as a child of seven or eight. Often, as adults, we have learned to mask our true selves in order to please other people, or we have gained the skills to round us out and strengthen our perceived weaknesses in order to become more like Jesus. (Jesus, of course, has *all* the strengths of all the personalities and *none* of the weaknesses.)

Our children's personality types were easier to discern in the "tweenager" time of life—from nine to thirteen. When Brock was about nine, we were teaching about personalities at our church's family camp. We were using Jim and Suzette Brawner's book *Taming the Family Zoo,* which uses animals to describe the different personalities. The choleric, a personality motivated by power, is a lion; the fun-loving sanguine is an otter; the diligent melancholic is a beaver; and the amiable phlegmatic is a golden retriever. When Brock took the test he came out even in two personalities, one being a lion. I said, "Let me take the test for you, Brock. I'll answer how I see you." The results were an overwhelming lion outcome. To which Brock replied, "I am not a lion! Don't tell me I am a lion. I will let you know what I am after I have decided!" (A *very* typical lion response!)

One of the best places to receive training on the personalities is through Florence Littauer's CLASS seminars. One year a counselor named Sue attended. She worked in a home for underprivileged, abused, and orphaned children. Upon return to her job, she began to categorize the children into personality types. She gave them a simple survey, and one of the questions was, "If you could be any kind of person in the world, what or who would you be?" Here are some of the answers she forwarded to Florence:

- The Populars wanted to be actors, comedians, TV stars in soap operas, cheerleaders, salesmen, Cinderella, or Miss Piggy.
- The Powerfuls wanted to be kings and queens, the president, Hitler, owners of big houses and limousines, highway patrolmen, and football players.

- The Perfects dreamed of being musicians, artist, poets, bankers, Mozart in *Amadeus,* and Garfield the cat.
- The Peacefuls wanted to be rich so they didn't have to work, live on lakes with boats and canoes, be golf pros, and have long vacations and more recess.

As she worked with the groups she found the Populars were motivated by abundant praise, the Powerfuls by appreciation of all their achievements, the Perfects by her encouragement and observation of how well they had done each task, and the Peacefuls by a slow building of a trusting relationship where they were finally convinced she valued them.[4]

The Powerful Personality

The powerful cholerics are extroverted, task oriented, decision makers, and natural leaders. Bob Phillips, author of *The Delicate Art of Dancing with Porcupines,* labels them drivers, and the DISC test, dominant. Their primary shortcomings are a lack of empathy and their bulldozer mentality. They are so focused on the task at hand they can sometimes run over people to get it done. They are primarily motivated by power. Fun to them is anything *they* decide on. The best way to motivate a choleric is to give him or her choices. This Powerful personality loves to be the hero.

Brock wrote an obituary for himself as a part of a junior high English assignment:

> Brock William Farrel was a model father. He died while saving his daughter from a speeding car. His family was crossing the street in a crosswalk when a man in a white Porsche flew into the intersection. The driver did not see the pedestrians and almost hit Brock's little girl. Before the car hit her, Brock pushed her out of the way and took a direct hit from the car. He died five hours later in the hospital. "Life is 10 percent what happens to us and 90 percent how we react"—Vince Lombardi. I think Brock acted the right way!

We were amazed that one short paragraph could provide so many clues into Brock's personality. He was a model father. Of course—model fathers make all the right decisions. He died a hero's death, providing for the safety of a loved one with quick-thinking action. He was hit by a white Porsche—a typical choleric would say there are only a few real power and prestige cars, and if you're going to go out, you might as well go out in style! He quoted Vince Lombardi, one of the winningest football coaches in history. Then to make sure no one would get it wrong, he told us he made the right decision!

The Popular Personality

The other extrovert is the people-oriented sanguine. Brawner labels these people otters because they love to have fun. Phillips calls them expressive; the DISC, inspirational.

They are creative, spontaneous, and have super people skills! They can lack perseverance (if it isn't fun, why stay at it?). And they love a party, so they can seem shallow and flippant to some of the other personalities. They are primarily motivated by people and praise. All they want is a little attention—okay, a lot of attention—and they will do anything to get it. If you want to motivate a sanguine, hook a task to a person or make it a party, and they are there for you! It is important with this Popular personality to find positive ways for them to get the attention they crave.

Zach has this personality style. When our friend Debe cast him as the lead role in the school Christmas play, everyone thought she had lost her mind. Zach, when he was in kindergarten, ran from the science fair to throw up just because he was supposed to hold up his insect collection and say one sentence about it! But Debe could tell he was flamboyant, liked to be the center of attention, and was funny. He had just always felt that he might let someone down if he were to play a lead role, and to Zachery nothing could be worse than to let down someone he loves. For years, our goal was to convince him that if he was just who God made him, he'd never let us down. So when he was cast as the pharaoh and got to be a comedian, make people laugh, and please his drama teacher and Mom and Dad—he was in heaven! All Debe had to do was tell him, "Zach, you are the best person for this part. I don't have anyone else who can come close to doing this part the way it needs to be done." The more Zach played the part, the more positive praise he received. By the end of the production, he was asked to do a promo piece at our Sunday morning worship service. He even added in a line and, in character as the pharaoh, gave directions to his father, who was standing in the pulpit! The congregation loved it, and the laughter just boosted his little ego all the more!

I (Pam) have this personality trait, so I can easily understand why Zach makes some of the decisions he makes. I can also understand what will wound his spirit and set him back from achieving his potential. The people-pleaser aspect of this personality can cause severe paralysis. My main goal as Zach's mother is to help him tune in to how he can please God. Otherwise, he will be tossed back and forth by public opinion, or he will be frozen, afraid to risk because he might not please someone. However, when people with these personalities sense that they are pleasing to God, they can become very effective in the kingdom because of their great people skills and persuasive ability.

The Peaceful Personality

The phlegmatic, or Brawner's retriever, is an introverted, no frills, peace-at-all-costs, likeable guy or gal. Phillips labels these as amiable; the DISC says they are steady. Everybody loves the Peaceful personality. Everyone gets along with retrievers because their goal in life is to not rock the boat. Everyone likes them—unless you want something done, you need a decision, or you are in a hurry. Then they can drive you crazy! Caleb is a blend of the Peaceful and the Perfect personality styles.

Caleb is impossible to rush in the morning. His favorite place to be is right next to Mom or Dad. And I mean *right next to.* He is like glue. He is a hug waiting to happen. He lives to make other people happy, and he is happiest when he feels emotionally close and connected to those he loves.

I got a clue about this when he was three and we were driving around town. I was preoccupied by some discouraging news I had received. Caleb was sitting next to me in his car seat. He's a perceptive little guy. He said, "Mommy, what's wrong?"

Knowing the content of my problem was well over his head, I just said, "I have something on my mind, and I want to talk to Daddy about it."

"Where's Daddy?"

"Honey, he's in a meeting."

"Daddy is always in a meeting."

"Yes, that's a lot of what pastors do. They meet with people, talk with them about their problems, and help them find God's plans."

"When will Daddy not be in meetings?"

"I don't know, honey—"

"I do," he interrupted. "When all the people in the world are dead. Then there won't be any more meetings!"

His candor caught me off guard, and I couldn't help but laugh out loud. To which Caleb replied, "See, I knew I could make you happy."

I am also married to a man whose personality is Peaceful. All that a Peaceful personality needs in life is to be appreciated. I know I could not do what I do as a leader, speaker, and writer if Bill weren't in my life. He really is the wind beneath my wings. Even while writing this book I told him, "Honey, I need you. You are my inspiration," and I meant it. People just function better with a little TLC, and the Peaceful personalities can give emotional support well.

The theme song of the Peaceful person would be Aretha Franklin's R-E-S-P-E-C-T! All they want is a little respect. When you show appreciation and respect to these people, they will do almost anything for you. They might take a while, but they will get it done.

This personality has a strange side, and I (Bill) feel like I can talk about it because this is my primary temperament. A child with this personality does not like to be defined by what he or she does. We saw this in Caleb's life early in school. His grades were below the level we were confident he could achieve, so we put together a plan for him to raise his GPA.

He began working the plan, and as his grades improved, we said to him, "You are *doing* awesome. You've been diligent with homework and have followed the plan well. We are so proud of how you have performed."

When Caleb's next progress report came home, his grades were down again. We were confused because we had established a good plan, he was working the plan, and we had praised his positive behavior. But eventually we realized we had defined him by his performance and had drained his natural motivation.

We changed our tactics with him from that day forward. We began saying to him, "Caleb, we want you to get the best grades you possibly can, but we want you to always remember that regardless of your grades, our lives are better simply because you are around." Kids with this personality would rather have you compliment their character than notice their achievements.

The Perfect Personality

The melancholy personality is introverted and task oriented. Most great artists and musicians have this personality. They are creative, and they want things done right. They have the patience to do things with excellence. Their attention to detail can drive other people, primarily the sanguine, crazy. The sanguine's response to a melancholy will always be, "Lighten up!" But they can't lighten up. The world is black-and-white and is in desperate need of fixing to these folks. They can become negative and depressed because they see the glass half empty and notice all the little undone things in the world.

The Brawner model calls these people beavers because they are hardworking and get the job done. The DISC test calls them cautious, and Bob Phillips labels them as analytical. They are always thinking, processing. When Brock was younger, I thought he might have this trait because he was so good at academics. But as he has gotten older, I see the lion's attitude that "the end justifies the means" coming out in him more often. Melancholics can never bring themselves to cut corners.

Bill is my editor. Because I am sanguine and choleric, I can create ideas by the boatload. I think all of them are brilliant, of course, just because I came up with them. I want to set sail with a host of ideas. Bill is my rudder in life, helping me to sort through the ideas, choose the best ones, and make them rise to the level of excellence. Without him, my impatient personality (which comes from *both* of my temperaments) would make many mistakes—possibly a few tragic ones.

Parenting a melancholy can be a mixed bag. They will always be the ones with a clean room, but they might be obsessive about it. One friend of mine with a melancholy son finally got a lock to put on the outside of his door because he could tell if someone had walked into his room! My sister has a little melancholy in her—all her clothes had to hang on hangers that were the same color as the garments! (I was lucky if I remembered to hang mine up.) Sharing a room with her was great for me and horrible for her. Deney was constantly cleaning up behind me because she couldn't stand my haphazard ways. After all, who has time to organize a closet when there is a date to go on or a party to attend? Deney organized her books from tallest to smallest. She had bins and boxes for everything.

To motivate a melancholic, give them answers because they will ask, "Why do we have to do it? Why do we have to do it this way?" They like answers and structure. And don't deviate from the plan!

When you parent a Perfect, make very few promises, or you will lose credibility. The way to bring out the best in this child's heart is to create a plan and carry it out. Establish some rituals he or she can rely on.

People with this personality collect evidence. They are constantly adding up the facts of life as they perceive them. When they are collecting positive evidence about life, they will say things like, "Wow, life is good. Oh, it is getting even better. I can't believe how good God is." But more often they spend their energy collecting negative evidence about life. They will dwell on thoughts such as, "Life is hard. Oh no, it's getting even harder. It's even more difficult than I thought." This process has no natural bottom, so this child has the potential to spiral downward emotionally.

As soon as you are aware of this trait in your child, begin to establish a deliberate baseline for their emotions. The baseline represents or triggers a decision to change one's behavior. It may be a CD your child plays that helps turn his or her emotions. It may be a spoken phrase that causes you to stop what you are doing and talk things through with your child. It may be the decision to take a walk or engage in some other physical activity. It may be a verse from the Bible that you or your child read out loud when he or she begins to spiral downward. The key is to have the child choose a decision because emotions follow decisions. Too often we encourage our children to think about what they are doing when we notice this emotional free fall. The problem is that these kids are already overthinking!

A family asked me (Bill) if I would help them with their ten-year-old son who, in their opinion, had an anger problem. As I spoke with this young man, I concluded he was a beaver who was facing a number of negative experiences in his life. As he spiraled downward, he would reach a point of being overwhelmed and would respond by expressing anger. To help him get control of his emotions before he reached the anger point, we established a "stop, drop, and roll" for him. When he first started to feel anxious, he would say out loud, "Stop!" He would then drop to the ground, roll on his side three times ending up on his knees. He would then pray out loud, "God, what should I do next?" He was so excited about the idea, he made a poster for his refrigerator and another for his bathroom mirror to remind himself that he didn't have to let his emotions control him.

Understanding the Birth Order

In *The New Birth Order Book,* Dr. Kevin Leman offers a short quiz to help the reader get a quick grasp of birth order:

> Which of the following sets of personality traits fits you best?
>
> - Perfectionist, reliable, conscientious, list-maker, well-organized, hard-driving, natural leader, critical, serious, scholarly, logical, doesn't like surprises, loves computers.
>
> - Mediator, compromising, diplomatic, avoids conflict, independent, loyal to peers, many friends, a maverick, secretive, unspoiled.
>
> - Manipulative, charming, blames others, attention seeker, tenacious, people person, natural salesperson, precocious, engaging, affectionate, loves surprises.

- Little adult by age seven, very thorough, deliberate, high achiever, self-motivated, fearful, cautious, voracious reader, black-and-white thinker, uses "very," "extremely," "exactly" a lot, can't bear to fail, has very high expectations for self, more comfortable with people who are older or younger.

If you noted that the test seemed rather easy because A, B, and C listed traits of the oldest right on down to the youngest in the family, you are right. If you picked list A, it's a very good bet you are firstborn in your family. If you chose list B, chances are you are a middle child...If list C seemed to relate best to who you are, it's likely you are the baby in the family...But what about list D? It describes the only child.[5]

Reading Dr. Leman's complete work is a good idea because the traits of the birth order can be affected by the age difference between children, the sex of each child, the physical, mental, and emotional differences, sibling deaths, adoptions, the birth order of each parent, and the blending of families.

Dr. Leman has done extensive research in this area.

For example, statistics show that firstborns often fill positions of high authority or achievement. *Who's Who in America* or *American Men and Women in Science* both contain a high percentage of firstborns. You will also find them more than well represented among Rhodes scholars and university presidents. As for presidents and pastors, you guessed it, a great number of them are firstborns. The way I define firstborn, twenty-three of forty of U.S. Presidents (56 percent) have been firstborn or functional firstborns.[6]

Twenty-three of the first 25 astronauts sent into space by the United States were firstborns. "At the other end of the birth order scale, you will find a lot of later borns who are comedians!"[7]

The second child sees the older sibling as stronger, smarter, and bigger and will usually shoot off in a completely different direction from that of his or her sibling. The key is to provide direction so the second child doesn't look at his or her supposedly perfect and high-achieving sibling and decide the only identity is to be the black sheep of the family. Parents who make a conscientious effort to help each child see his or her uniqueness and value will be able to find a positive outlet for the second sibling.

In our family, when Zach entered junior high, he took up skateboarding. His older brother was totally inept at the sport, which made the sport even more attractive to Zach. He wrote all his English papers about skateboarding. His science fair project was about skateboarding. He wore skater clothing and he even launched his own line of "Zeek" wear. (The clothing motto was "Don't be a geek, wear Zeek!") He even designed his own business cards for the company. We made sure he kept up his other interests—football, friendships, and guitar lessons—but he definitely identified with the skater crowd. We were careful to not allow him to "hang" with skaters. If he was going to skate, he was going to do it legally, safely, and competitively. Even though a few of our friends were concerned that all Zach wanted to talk about was skating, we knew at this point in time he needed something he felt he was really great at. And he was a really good skater. Zach wanted to be great at something in which Brock did not excel. They were so close in age that he needed a strong reason to not dwell in Brock's shadow as he entered high school.

We even weighed various high school options for Zach and talked with him about whether he felt he could make his own mark if he attended the same school as his brother. In the end, Zach felt he had his own set of strengths that were different from his brother's, and he chose to attend the same high school because they really are good friends.

The youngest children have an insatiable desire for attention (maybe because they have to fight for attention under the shadow of so many siblings, or maybe because they are used to attention, being the "baby" of the family). This desire for attention makes the youngest child bold enough to try almost anything. Dr. Leman, the youngest in his family, says, "We just go ahead and *do it* and worry about the repercussions later."[8]

Here is a thumbnail sketch of considerations parents can make based on birth order:

Firstborns need a break! Because they are already hard on themselves, you don't need to be so hard on them. Because of their intense approach to life, you might want to go overboard in teaching them people skills like tact, empathy, and compassion to balance out the achiever in them. If they are also only children, expose them to relationships so they can learn important people skills like sharing, caring, peer-level interaction, and negotiation. Both firstborn and only children feel an intrinsic need to be perfect, so let them see your flaws and the way you handle failure.

Middle children need understanding. Give your middle children space to explore their feelings, their options, and their identity. If you have several middle children, don't let them get lost in the shuffle. Help them identify and develop their own unique gifts. Don't let everything in their life be hand-me-down. They have natural people skills, so encourage their use. They may want more social time away from the family, and that's all right. With other people they can feel like the top dog.

Youngest children need structure. Give your last born discipline and try to keep the same family rules. Even if you try to parent the same, you will naturally be a little easier on the last born just because you are more relaxed in your role as a parent. Don't make things too easy for the last born. Help them excel academically because everyone in the family is smarter than them just because of age. They have the confidence to tackle big challenges, so let them. Don't squelch their dreams.

Understanding How They Learn

We highly recommend Cynthia Tobias' *The Way They Learn.* Cynthia, an educator, describes how children perceive the world and process information. She describes children's learning styles in four categories:

1. *Concrete sequential:* those who are conventional, accurate, hardworking, factual, organized, and consistent learners;
2. *Abstract sequential:* those who analyze well because they are structured, objective, logical, and systematic;

3. *Abstract random:* those who are sensitive, compassionate, and imaginative and also prefer to be spontaneous and flexible; and

4. *Concrete random:* those who are intuitive, curious, creative, instructive, adventurous—but realistic.[9]

Three Weddings, Three Personalities!

Carol Rischer and I were to teach at a women's retreat that was in a remote community along the California coast, so we decided to drive the seven hours together. When we talked about raising kids, she entertained me for hours as she described the differences in her three beautiful daughters' weddings. Here's a condensed picture of just how personality and birth order can combine for some very unique weddings!

"Melanie is our choleric-melancholy mix. She is type A, responsible, and firstborn. She planned her wedding to neatly follow six weeks after her university graduation. The production was elegant, formal, sophisticated, and dramatic—as is our Melanie. Her gown was elaborate, well beaded with ornate long sleeves and an appropriately dramatic long train. Her music featured a classical string quartet plus a trumpeter playing a trumpet voluntary as her processional. Melanie's pastor daddy officiated and included a tearful presentation from him of a pearl necklace to remind her of her value. The bride and the groom sang beautifully to each other in the tradition of her parents (that would be my husband and me back in 1969). The wedding dinner/dance/reception was poolside at a formal hotel setting where the surrounding hillside mountains were part of the planned backdrop for our out-of-town guests. Graciousness reigned. God balanced Melanie's responsible personality with a patient and nurturing psychologist husband who continues to listen, level, and lead in their Christian marriage.

"Cheryl, our sanguine, fun-loving middle child planned a wedding celebration that was entitled 'The Wedding of a Gentleman and a Princess' and was scripted on the PowerPoint screens above the sanctuary. Cheryl's curiosity and flair for adventure led her to her man on a Christian singles website. Two adventuresome, godly Christian virgins somehow found each other! Cheryl's bridesmaids did a little skip dance step down the aisle to the jazzy 'It Had to Be You,' and Cheryl twirled down the aisle in her beaded, off-the-shoulder princess gown with her daddy's arm raised above her head. Her music was a jazz combo—trumpet, keyboard, drums, guitar, bass—performed by professionals who added zest and vitality to an already exciting story. Cheryl surprised her groom at the reception by sitting him on a chair on the dance floor and singing to him Shania Twain's 'Any Man of Mine.' Rob surprised Cheryl with a dance rendition of a *Men in Black* routine with his guy friends. God knew Cheryl's 'life's a party' outlook would best be balanced with a stable corporate defense attorney who loves the Lord and his sparkling bride!" (Note the change from wedding number one to wedding number two. Those second children don't want to fall into their older siblings' perfect shadow. Cheryl created a memory completely different from Melanie's. The sanguine in her made the day one few people would ever forget!)

"Deanna, who is a phlegmatic, type B, nothing-is-worth-stressing-about baby of the family, married only 11 days after she arrived home from her university graduation and choir tour. She knew all the details would be taken care of—why wouldn't we all want to help her?—and that her wedding would be perfect. The stage was dramatic, with a dozen hand-painted pillars surrounded by a sea of candles. Deanna floated down the aisle—smiling and genuinely relaxed—in her simple but gorgeous gown—with her groom waiting anxiously for his life mate and ministry mate. They sang, emotionally but professionally, 'From This Moment.' Since they are both performers, both confident, they were both ready to enjoy every minute of the day and the rest of their lives. Their music was classic jazz with professional sax, bass, and piano. The dinner dance was a celebration for all to enjoy—no uptight stuff for them. God let the PK (pastor's kid) become a PW (pastor's wife) who will survive because she doesn't sweat the small stuff. She lets others worry about what they want to. The crowds cheered and blew bubbles as their limo drove off with the couple standing and waving to their fans through the sunroof. Life is to be enjoyed!" (Note the last born style. She knew everyone would want to help pull her wedding together in a short amount of time. The babies of the family can be very responsible like Deanna, but they also might take risks like pulling together a wedding from the road. Deanna was on tour just prior to her wedding! Last borns who have a winning family know they have a terrific team who will all pull together to make the event wonderful. Last borns know the system and work the system, and because they are so easy to be around and are such natural people people, everyone usually really enjoys being a part of their lives even if they have to do a little bit of the work.)

Cynthia also explains three educational terms for the way children best learn a body of information:

1. *Auditory learners* are those who remember information best if they hear it. These children do best if they have parents who...

   - offer to drill them verbally
   - help them put information into rhythmic patterns, like a song or rap
   - let them read aloud
   - minimize visual distractions in the study area
   - say the vital information out loud

2. *Visual learners* are those who remember best if they have seen the information, not just heard it. These children perform best if their parents...

   - give them bright colors and large spaces to draw or write
   - encourage them to doodle or take notes while listening
   - let them underline or highlight in a book or draw symbols or pictures they can associate with vital facts or figures
   - provide charts, pictures, and graphs that help log the information in their minds

3. *Kinesthetic learners* learn by experience or touch. These children learn more easily if they...
  - take frequent breaks while studying
  - can write and draw in large spaces
  - hear stories aloud that have lots of action
  - move while learning, act out material, or even pace while memorizing[10]

As the parent of a kinesthetic learner (Zach), we can tell you traditional classrooms for the most part are not set up well to enhance their learning. Sitting still in class with an emphasis on textbooks and worksheets is not very effective with these active learners. Hands-on learning activities work better but are not common in most classrooms, so you might have to go out of your way to provide alternatives and options to help your child learn. We built skate ramps to learn math. Zach and Mom would go on walks where we talked through projects, papers, and test data. We bought all kinds of games to learn spelling, reading, math, history, and social studies information. Pulling in art and music seemed to add to Zach's ability to learn.

These learners can seem uncooperative in a classroom, but with some creative parenting and creative teachers, these children can excel.

Understanding How They Perceive Love

Often as children become adults, they express frustration about certain choices their parents might have made. In families with several children, one episode might be *interpreted* many ways. The *perception* of love is as relevant to a child as the foundation of love itself. Children feel loved in a variety of ways. Gary Chapman describes five love languages: words of affirmation, physical touch, quality time, acts of service, and gifts.[11] Of course, every person enjoys all these expressions of love; however, one or two might mean more to each of your children.

Chapman suggests three main tools to discover your child's love language: questions, observation, and experimentation. "Questions may be your greatest ally...you might ask, 'If you really wanted to show your grandmother you loved her, how would you do it?'" A child's or teen's answer might be a reflection of what speaks love to him or her. Chapman continues, "Look for ways in which he expresses love or appreciation to others. Keep notes on what you observe...Observe also the complaints of the teenager. What a person complains about is a clue to his or her primary love language."[12] Finally, Chapman says that a third way to discover a teenager's primary love language is to experiment by focusing on one of the five love languages each week and observing the teen's response. All in all, you can't go wrong if you parent by using all the love languages with all your children—then you are bound to be speaking love to each child somehow, someway!

Caught You Being Good

One goal of parenthood is to help children see themselves the way God does. They need to understand that despite their shortcomings, Jesus would have died for them even if they were the only people on earth. This is quite different, however, from the inflated view some current educational methods might produce. For example, it does a child no favors to never give Ds or Fs. If a child is failing in a course, the parent, child, and teacher need a plan to address the problem. The answer should include a realistic evaluation of the child's potential and performance with identifiable steps to make improvement. This is much better than pretending the problem doesn't exist for fear of hurting his or her feelings. When that child gets out into the real world, an employer isn't going to stroke the child's ego just to get a job completed.

Children deserve to discover their strengths so they can focus on developing those talents for their future. Likewise, they deserve to uncover their weaknesses so they can create a plan to fortify and shore up those areas. Here are two great ideas from Emilie Barnes: In her More Hours in My Day seminars, Emilie explains how she gives stickers that say, "Caught You Being Good" to her grandchildren. She also has reward coupons that a parent can give for a job well done.[13]

Decision Point
Be a Student of Your Child

As you discover your child's personality, gifts, talents, and learning styles, you'll want to encourage your child in those areas. Look for ways to celebrate your children and the treasure inside each.

There are many ways to praise your child for being good and for a job well done. Here are a few ways we praised our kids:

- *Celebrate the mundane.* Hand out Popsicles after the room is cleaned.

- *Celebrate the successes.* From riding a bike without training wheels to passing the driver's exam, significant steps in life deserve a party.

- *Celebrate the potential.* Rejoice whenever your kids go to friends' homes or someplace new. Instead of voicing our fears with instructions such as, "Don't goof off. Be sure to say please and thank you. Don't fight," voice your faith. "I know I'll hear a great report. I bet when I pick you up I'm going to hear what a great helper you were. I bet they tell me what great manners you have. I can't wait for them to see what a great son I have!" (And our kids usually went the extra mile because they wanted to hear the good report.)

- *Celebrate character.* Give out your own set of awards for such traits as kindness, helpfulness, and sympathy.

SEVEN

Decide to Partner with God
Unleashing Potential Through Prayer

∾∾∾

I (Pam) have several prayer notebooks where I keep track of requests. Recently, I taught a six-week session called A Woman's Prayer Project. We each gathered photos of those we loved and created scrapbook pages for each person. We added verses to pray over each person and our requests, hopes, and dreams for each one. It was a fun project that we each use now in our daily devotions.

I would encourage you to create a prayer book with photos of your children and requests you are praying for each child. Add verses to pray along with the requests.

Fern Nichols, founder of Moms In Touch, presented a photo album, complete with all the verses, requests, and answers, to each of her children. It was the first thing each child packed as they left for college and became a wonderful, natural tool for sharing their faith on campus.

Swap Kid Concerns

If you continue to make the same prayer request for your child over and over for years and years, you could easily begin to believe the lie, "Why bother? Nothing's ever going to change." If you are feeling that way, try praying with another mom who has been praying for her own child for a long time. Believing that God will move is easier when you aren't as emotionally drained as you are for your own child. It's even easier to pray when the requests are different. Maybe you are praying for a prodigal daughter, and your friend has a son who hasn't made a decision for Christ yet. If you see change in the life of your friend's child, your own faith may be renewed. When you don't see immediate results, you may be tempted to think something is wrong with your prayers. Exchanging requests can sometimes bolster your own faith and give you renewed strength to go the distance with your own child.

Much of our faith in God and belief in the power of prayer has come from parents who have remained strong in times of crisis. In our role in the pastorate, we stood clutching their hands as they said goodbye at a graveside. We were a sounding board when they had to make tough decisions about surgeries, schooling, and sending their kids down the aisle. We sat in classrooms, courtrooms, counseling rooms, and waiting rooms. We saw how *strong* God can be on behalf of a parent. One of our favorite verses is 2 Timothy 2:13: "If we are faithless, he will remain faithful, for he cannot disown himself."

Over and over we have witnessed the faithfulness of God. We think one of the best gifts a parent can ever give a child is to have a strong personal faith in God, so that when our children need us to believe God for something big in their lives, we have the faith to stand with them.

One of my (Pam's) favorite examples of a parent with strong faith is my friend Julie. Her daughter Sarah was born with her skull only partially developed. All babies have soft spots, but Sarah's was much worse. It refused to close. Doctors weren't sure Sarah would live. But she was a fighter, and she pulled through. For most of Sarah's life, Julie had to make sure that Sarah never bumped her head and never cried. Now *that* is stress!

When Sarah was about three, she had to have major surgery. Julie and her family attended our church, so many of us gathered for a prayer and worship service on Sarah's behalf. We also coordinated a prayer chain. Julie gave each of us a prayer card for her daughter. Each card had a picture of Sarah on it and a Bible verse that Julie asked that we pray for Sarah each time we looked at it. I placed mine on the refrigerator, where it has remained to this day. I still pray for Sarah even though she is a beautiful blonde walking miracle. She is now a wonderful teenager and has survived numerous surgeries and hospital stays. God's faithfulness has allowed her to find a way to live a normal life.

A parent of less faith might have coddled or spoiled such a sick child, but Julie has integrated Sarah into everyday life. Sarah can never be without one of her parents because her medical condition is so complicated and tenuous. She cannot be bumped or hit, so there is no roughhousing for her. She cannot participate in an activity where she could fall. But if you met her, you would never know this. She is vivacious, sweet, personable, and sings like an angel.

Parents of special-needs children have moments, crises of faith, where they are at a crossroads. They can become bitter and angry at God and question, "Why us?" Or they can reach out by faith for the hem of Christ's garment and trust that some of His power might be available on behalf of their family. Julie has done that. Her faith is like a giant sequoia tree. It is silent, majestic, and strong. Being around her is like gazing at the base of those giant, beautiful trees with a sense of awe and wonder at the God who could create something so beautiful yet so strong.

In *The Power of a Praying Parent*, Stormie Omartian writes this:

> We don't have to pace the floor anxiously, biting our nails, cracking our knuckles, dreading the terrible twos or tortuous teens. We don't have to live in fear of what each new development may bring, what dangers might be lurking behind every corner. Nor do we have to be perfect parents.

> We can start right now—this very minute, in fact—making
> a positive difference in our child's future. It's never too early
> and it's never too late…The key is not trying to do it all by
> ourselves all at once, but rather turning to the expert parent
> of all time—our Father God—for help…There is great *power*
> in doing that, far beyond what most people imagine.[1]

We have found that more than anything else, prayer accomplishes a change in us! That's why I (Pam) have decided to pray before I *push*, pray before I *panic*, pray before I *pressure*. One of the mothers in my prayer circle reminds herself, "Pray it, don't say it!"

If and when God leads you to confront a situation, you will act and react in a godlier way if you have consistently prayed first. Starting with an active prayer life gives God the opportunity to parent through you. Prayer turns your heart into a vessel of His love and discernment. To remind me of my commitment to pray first, I often wear a bracelet that says, P.U.S.H. (Pray Until Something Happens).

Personalizing Prayer

One of our favorite ways to pray is to pray Scripture, personalizing it for the child we are praying for. There are a couple of ways to do this. One is very simple. Just choose a portion of Scripture (the psalms work well) that addresses some of the areas you are concerned about for your son or daughter.

For example, the night before Brock's football games in high school, I (Pam) would pray a section of Psalm 91 over Brock:

> Brock, who dwells in the shelter of the Most High, will rest
> in the shadow of the Almighty. Brock will say of the Lord,
> "He is my refuge and my fortress, my God, in whom I trust."
> Surely God will save him from the fowler's snare and from
> the deadly pestilence. He will cover Brock with His feathers,
> and under His wings he will find refuge; His faithfulness will
> be Brock's shield and rampart…If Brock makes the Most
> High his dwelling—even the Lord, who is his refuge—then
> no harm will befall him, no disaster will come near his
> tent. For He will command His angels concerning Brock,

to guard him in all his ways… "Because Brock loves me," says the Lord, "I will rescue him; I will protect him, for he acknowledges My name. He will call upon Me, and I will answer him; I will be with him in trouble, I will deliver him and honor him."

The other option is to create a composite of verses that fortifies an area of weakness. If you have a concordance, you can look up verses that address your need. For example, all of our children have been afraid of the dark or have had nightmares. We have taught them how to take their stand in Christ and say, "In the name of Jesus and His shed blood on the cross, I command any evil spirits to be silenced and sent away." Then we encourage them to pray the truth about God's power, victory, and ability to overcome (inserting their name in the blanks):

> You, dear_____, are from God and have overcome them, because the one who is in you is greater than the one who is in the world (1 John 4:4). For He has rescued _____ from the dominion of darkness and brought _____ into the kingdom of the Son He loves (Colossians 1:13). I have told you these things, so that in Me you may have peace. In this world you will have trouble. But take heart! I have overcome the world (John 16:33). I write to _____ because you are strong, and the Word of God lives in you, and you have overcome the evil one (1 John 2:14). With God we will gain the victory, and He will trample down our enemies (Psalm 108:13). Thanks be to God! He gives _____ the victory through our Lord Jesus Christ (1 Corinthians 15:57). Everyone born of God overcomes the world. This is the victory that has overcome the world, even our faith (1 John 5:4).

Experiencing the Power of Prayer

We love to pray using God's Word because we never know when we might need it. I (Pam) had begun to pray for Caleb before he was born, but my biggest answer to prayer for him was quite dramatic. It was life changing for all of us.

I had been out running errands. As I walked into the house the phone was ringing—it was the phone call no mother ever wants to receive. "Pam," said a voice I barely recognized as Bill's. He sounded scared, and he struggled with his words… "The sheriff wants you to bring as many photos of Caleb as you can find. Honey, the boys are missing."

I hung up the phone and burst into tears. My Caleb was only five years old! How could he be missing? He had been at his best friend's house playing, and now he and his little friend were gone.

I looked around for photos of Caleb but I couldn't see any. My eyes blurred with tears of panic. "God, Caleb needs me right now. I need to find pictures. Please be with my Caleb, and help me be the kind of mom he needs. Give me Your peace."

A supernatural calm came over me, and as I looked up I saw photos of Caleb all over the wall and albums of them on the shelf. I grabbed them and ran out the door.

As I headed across town, I panicked again. "Oh, God, what was he wearing? What did I put on him this morning?" I couldn't remember. "I must be a terrible mother! I can't even remember what I put on my little boy! God, I need Your peace! I can't think. Please help me be the kind of mom Caleb needs. Help me remember. Give me peace so I can think. What did I put on him for kindergarten? Protect Caleb; give him peace."

Then I remembered: striped shirt, black sweatpants, brown boots. Tears puddled in my eyes and overflowed down my cheeks. I blinked and frantically wiped my eyes because I couldn't see the road.

"Lord, give me Your peace. Help me make it to Gail's."

I thought of my friend Gail, and I empathized with how frantic she must be feeling as well. What would I say to her? I knew she was a great mom, attentive and caring. "She's as freaked out as I am right now," I thought. "God, what am I going to say to Gail? Give her peace. Help me be the kind of friend I need to be right now. Be with our two little boys. Give them Your peace."

As I turned the corner, I saw Gail in the center of her yard. I parked the car and ran to wrap my arms around her. "Gail, I love you. We will get through this together. We'll pray, and God will find those boys." We begged God to watch over our children and to give us peace so we could think. Patrol cars were speeding to the scene, and Bill appeared from behind the house. "Not there, either." Then he saw me. He wrapped his arms around me and he prayed, "God, help us find our precious Caleb."

The sheriff interrupted. "We are dispatching all available squad cars and two helicopters. Are those the pictures of your children?" He asked a few more questions and then said, "We would like one parent of each child to stay with me at the command post." Bill suggested that the mothers stay, and he volunteered to lead the charge into the countryside of overgrown brush.

My older two boys spread the word to the kids coming off school buses, and soon more worried parents appeared from their homes to help in the search. When Brock and Zach returned, I sent one of my best friends home with them in case Caleb was going to try to make it home, five miles away. As they pulled from the curb, I could see their worried faces peering back at me. They were trying to be brave, but I knew they were anxious. As I watched the van pull around the corner and out of my sight, I was distressed because now I couldn't see anyone in my family. Even though I knew my older boys would be safe with my friend, panic and fear began to rise again. "Lord, please give Brock and Zach peace. I can't see them or Bill, and they can't see me. And Caleb can't see any of us! We all need Your peace!"

The sheriff in command said, "Mrs. Farrel, what time is it?" I told him. Two hours had already elapsed. Two helicopters appeared overhead. They announced like a booming voice from heaven, "Two missing youths, age five. Caleb Farrel..." Then they announced a description of each. I looked at Gail. Tears were streaming down both our faces. This was like a nightmare, but it was real.

"God, be with Caleb. I know Your Word. You say You hem him in before and behind. You hold all things in the palm of Your hand. You say that all the angels are at Your command. Send Your angels. Put a hedge of protection around those boys. Be with my Caleb. He knows You. Your Spirit resides inside him. Give him Your peace. Wrap Your love around him. And be with Bill too. Give him Your peace."

I pictured Bill, walking through the tall brush around our city. Helicopters hovered overhead just as they did in the images from Vietnam

I had grown up seeing. Men died there. I came face-to-face with my worst fears and again prayed for Caleb. "Let Your presence be a shelter to him. Lord, You say You shelter us under Your wings—shelter Caleb. You say You are a fortress and a deliverer—deliver Caleb." I shook my head and prayed, "God, give me Your peace. Help me be the kind of mom I need to be. It won't help anyone if I break down. Give me Your peace, Your strength, Your hope. Give me *YOU!*"

A supernatural calm reassured my heart. I began to pray specifically for Caleb, imagining how he must feel.

"Mrs. Farrel, what time is it?" I told the officer. Now three hours had passed. I began to cry as I sensed the precious time ebbing away.

I prayed, "God, You know all things. I take my stand in You and Your shed blood on the cross. I command all evil be sent away through Your power." The peace returned, and I continued to pray for Caleb and direct the stream of new volunteers that kept arriving.

"Mrs. Farrel, what time is it?"

I wanted to scream, "Get a watch!" But I didn't. I prayed, "Help me be the kind of citizen I need to be right now." So I looked at my watch and again told the officer the time.

"It's been four hours. If we don't find the boys in the next few minutes, we'll have to go down the street to the fire station and set up a permanent command post."

The words slapped me in the face. I knew what that meant, and it was not good news. I'd seen all the John Walsh films. I had shown *Stranger Danger* and similar videos to my children. This was bad news. This was the loss of hope. This was the beginning of the end.

"God, You say You are in control, and I believe that. I am going to decide right now that regardless of what happens, I will hang on to You. I've seen families go through tragedy. The families that make it have chosen You. I know that the only hope and help for my family is to believe You are who You say You are. Lord, Your Word says You are good. It says You can turn dark into light and work all things together for good, so right now I am choosing to believe that. And even if they bring my precious Caleb to me dead across their arms, I will choose to believe the truth of who You are. It is the only hope. I can choose despair or I can choose You. I choose You. Give us Your presence—

Caleb, Bill, Brock, Zach, and me. I am claiming and standing in Your peace."

A voice shook me from my daze of prayer. I saw a squad car pull up and two officers talking. The commander approached, "We have received a sighting of two youths. We are sending a squad car by to see if the two children are your sons. We don't yet have confirmation..."

I smiled and said, "But we have hope." The time...ticked...slowly... by...so Gail and I prayed some more together, and God held us together with His peace. About 20 minutes later, a squad car pulled up. Two doors popped open and out tumbled two tousled, dirty, ragtag boys—*our boys!* I ran to my son, wrapped my arms around him, and said, "I love you, Caleb!"

I heard a quiet but relieved, "I love you, Mommy." Bill had run back at the news. He gave Caleb a hug, they both said "I love you," and then we asked, "Where have you been?"

The story goes something like this: Caleb's kindergarten class was sometimes released earlier than the upper grades, so Caleb and his friend would often go to each other's homes to play and then return back to school when their siblings' classes were finished. That's what had happened on this day. Caleb and his friend were eating fresh-baked cookies on Gail's front patio when Gail went in to get the last batch of cookies out of the oven. She returned in just a few moments, but the boys were gone.

While Gail was frantically looking for the boys, Bill arrived at school to drive the kids home. When he didn't see Caleb and his friend, he called Gail, and she said, "I can't find the boys. I've looked everywhere. I've just called the police." Bill went immediately to Gail's, where the police had already arrived. That's when he called me.

It seems that Caleb's friend had said to Caleb, "You want to go on an adventure?" It was a simple game they played at school. They would simply march around the property, pretending to be on an adventure. Caleb said sure, and off they went—around the corner and down a few blocks. They came across some playground equipment at an apartment complex on their journey and played there for a while. The boys then looked up, and Caleb's friend saw a mobile home park across the street and said, "My babysitter lives there! Let's go see her." (His sitter actually lives in a mobile home park in another city!) They waited at the light at the busiest four-lane road in our community, and when it turned green they sped across the street. They played in some people's yards and then went underground into a huge storm tunnel. That's where they were for all those hours.

Eventually they popped their heads out from the storm drain. The manager of the mobile home park, a kindly grandmother, had rallied the retirees of the park, and everyone was out looking for our two boys. When she saw them, she said, "Now boys, I think your parents are very worried about you. Why don't we get into my golf cart and go call the police so you can get back to them?"

My son piped up, "Oh ma'am, we can't get in your golf cart. You're a stranger." (He can totally run away from home for more than four hours when he's never even been allowed to go out of the front yard before, but he remembers to say no to strangers!) Just then, a parent from our school drove in the park and saw what was happening. He got out of the car with his daughter, whom they knew, and said, "Hi, guys. You know us—why don't we *all* get in the golf cart and go call the police?"

That was the longest day of our lives. We have a new appreciation for the grace God gives when we need it because somehow He put a peace in our hearts that, to this day, we still cannot explain. We are different parents because of that day. And Caleb is a different young man. A few days after his ninth birthday, Caleb said to me, "Mom, last weekend, did you share with the women at the retreat the story of when I got lost?"

"Yes, honey. It helps their faith in God grow."

"Like it did mine. It's like God saved me for something important, and I just need to stay close to Him and He'll show me, right?"

"Right." *So right.*

God has a plan for Caleb and for your child and for you. We have experienced how He works all together for our good. We know God can get us through any parenting challenge. We have a sure confidence, a proven faith. We also treasure each and every moment. I (Pam) treasure the mundane task of folding a million sets of white athletic socks. I love to run my fingers through Caleb's curly hair. I get less frustrated over the small stuff, like plates left on the coffee table, burps, or the mountains of sneakers, cleats, and sports bottles that reappear across the living room each day. I treasure the privilege of just seeing each child, of serving each child, of praying for each child, and of being inconvenienced and annoyed by each child. The treasure is so much sweeter after coming so close to losing it.

Here are a few prayers we have prayed for our children. You can use these separately or as combined together to form a lifelong prayer for each of your children.

Prayer for Inner Strength

Lord, I pray that our children will love You with all their heart, soul, mind, and strength, and that Your Word will be on their hearts. Help us teach Your truths diligently as we sit in our house, when we walk, when we lie down, and when we rise up. Help us find ways to bind Your commandments as signs on their hands and on their foreheads. Give us creative ways to place Your statutes on our doorposts and on our gates (Deuteronomy 6:7-9). Help our children to be strong and very courageous, being careful to do all according to Your law. Do not let them turn from the left or the right, so they might have success wherever they go. Help them not to tremble or be dismayed, for You are with them wherever they go (Joshua 1:7-9). Let our family be like the people Joshua led, who said, "We will serve the LORD our God and obey him" (Joshua 24:24). Let Your gracious hand be on our children (Nehemiah 2:8) and let them be prepared for such a time as this (Esther 4:14). If they should ever have to risk all for You, let them say, "If I perish, I perish" (Esther 4:16). May they delight in Your law and meditate on it day and night. Make them like a tree firmly planted, which yields fruit in its season, and in whatever they do, may they prosper (Psalm 1:3). Let them know that You withhold no good thing from those who walk uprightly (Psalm 84:11 NASB). Help them continually set You before their eyes (Psalm 16:8).

Prayer for Wisdom

Show our children the path of life and assure them that in Your presence is fullness of joy and pleasures forever (Psalm 16:11). Lord, be their rock of refuge and a strong fortress (Psalm 31:2). Let them trust in You, do good, dwell in the land, and cultivate faithfulness. Let them delight themselves in You so You can give them the desires of their hearts. Help them commit their way to You (Psalm 37:3-5). Let them trust in You with all their hearts and not lean on their own understanding. In all their ways help them acknowledge You and look to You as You make their paths straight (Proverbs 3:5-6).

Prayer for Influence

But if they say, "I will not remember Him," let them feel like Jeremiah and say, "His word is in my heart like a fire...I am weary of holding it in...I cannot" (Jeremiah 20:9). Let them not shrink from declaring the whole counsel of God (Act 20:27 KJV).

I know these things will happen if they will present themselves to You as living and holy sacrifices and not be conformed to this world, but be transformed by the renewing of their minds (Romans 12:1-2). Let them be wise in what is good and innocent in what is evil (Romans 16:19). Let them be patient and kind, not jealous or arrogant or unloving. Help them rejoice in the truth (1 Corinthians 13:4-6). Let them be filled with Your Spirit so they experience the fruit of love, joy, peace, patience, kindness, goodness, faithfulness, gentleness, and self-control (Galatians 5:22). I pray that the eyes of their hearts will be enlightened so they will know the hope of Your calling, the riches of the glory of Your inheritance in the saints, and the surpassing greatness of Your power toward us who believe (Ephesians 1:18-19). Let them remember that they can do all things through You as You strengthen them (Philippians 4:13), and let me experience the joy of knowing that my children walk in the truth (3 John 4).

God Answers Prayer

We believe that keeping track of prayer requests now will encourage you in the future. Let me (Pam) share an example. I prayed this while I was pregnant with Brock:

"God, give him the faith of a Daniel or a Joseph. Give him the courage to stand for You—even the courage to stand alone for You. Make him a strong witness of light in this dark world. God, may many come to know You personally because of the life of this little one."

Here's a snapshot of how God has answered those prayers:

When Brock entered high school, he invited many of his friends to parties where he shared his personal testimony, explained the gospel, and then gave his friends opportunities to meet Christ. By the end of his freshman year, 34 of his friends had made decisions for Christ. Realizing we needed to help them continue to grow with God, we contacted the Fellowship of Christian Athletes and helped Brock launch a club on the campus during his sophomore year.

Before his junior year, Brock had attended an FCA camp where one of his FCA leaders, Derrick, was speaking. Brock was fascinated by Derrick's description of how he made Jesus known. Derrick explained that during his college football career he would yell out, "Jesus loves you!" any time he was at the bottom of a pile after making a tackle. He challenged the players to think of ways they might be more outspoken on campus the following year. That same summer, Brock had heard the reports that the Supreme Court had restricted football players from saying a prayer before a game in Texas. Brock thought that was a wrong decision, especially in light of the school shootings across the nation the prior spring. He often asked us questions such as "How can they expect kids to act well when they have taken the Ten Commandments off the walls and taken prayer off the campus?"

Brock decided he wanted to take a stand. He called up his buddies on the team and said, "This week, after we beat Fallbrook, I'm going to the 50-yard line to pray. Will you join me? I'm going to call all the guys and the other teams' FCA huddle. So, win or lose, can I count on you to be at the 50?" They all said, "You bet. We're there for ya, man!"

At the Moms In Touch prayer group that morning, I shared Brock's plan with the moms, and we prayed for all the guys, just as we'd prayed for them before every team outreach.

That opponent was expected to be the hardest they would meet all season, and they were. Brock's team lost 38–0. After the game, the team was discouraged, disappointed, and disillusioned. With heads down, the team wandered aimlessly to their locker room, but Brock went straight to the 50-yard line. He knelt down—all alone.

Some of us moms were huddled together, and Bill was standing nearby. My heart ached at the sight of my son kneeling alone at the 50. I said to Bill, "Honey, he's all alone! Should I go down and help him?"

I (Bill) turned to Pam and simply said, "A varsity quarterback does not want his mom to come on the field to help him with anything! He'll be all right."

Tears streamed down my cheeks—a mixture of empathy and pride. Then I remembered the prayer we had prayed years ago before Brock was born: "Help him stand alone for you, God." And now he was. God answers prayer!

Soon, three players from the opposing team joined Brock at the 50, and they prayed. After the game, Derrick, who was in the stands, went down to encourage Brock. Then another man who was a football head coach and who attends our church encouraged him. We gathered Brock's younger brothers together and made our way to the field.

I threw my arms around Brock's tall, sweaty body. Reaching up, I took his face in my hands and said, "I have never been more proud of you than I am at this moment. I know tonight was one of the hardest nights of your life. I know you are disappointed at the loss and disappointed that your team was distracted and didn't join you at the 50. But you kept your word to God. Those who honor God, God honors. Brock, I don't know how and I don't know when, but God will honor you for this."

The next weekend, I had a speaking engagement that took me out of town, so I asked Bill to have Brock call me from the field after his game. At 2:00 AM (eastern standard time) I got a call from California on my cell phone. "Mom, we won! And there were about 40 of us praying at the 50 tonight!"

I replied, "Those who honor God—"

"God honors," Brock completed the sentence.

God has continued to be true to His promise in Psalms 84:11 (NASB): "No good thing does He withhold from those who walk uprightly." As Brock has walked uprightly, God has sent good things—all answers to prayers. Brock's senior year he was named Athlete of the Year, he received the Scholar-Leader-Athlete award from the local chapter of the National Football Foundation and College Hall of Fame, he was named San Diego Citizen of the Year (and that came with a commendation from the governor and a scholarship from the local chapter of the NFL Retired Player's Association). He was also given our high school's highest award for servant leadership, Knight of the Year. *God answers prayer!*

Decision Point
Partner with God in Parenting

You can't give away what you don't own. To partner with God, you'll need to get to know God. Decide what the next step will be in developing your relationship with God individually and as a couple so your children can lean on your faith and learn from you as they develop their own.

1. Make sure you know Christ personally. Below is a statement of love from God to you. Read it alone and then as a family, and make sure each person is connected to the God who created him or her.

   "I love you and have a plan for you."

   - I came in order that you might have life—life in all its fullness (John 10:10 GNT).

   - I came so they can have real and eternal life, more and better life than they ever dreamed of (John 10:10 MSG).

   - God love the world so much that he gave his only Son, so that everyone who believes in him may not die, but have eternal life (John 3:16 GNT).

   "Sin has broken our relationship, and you are separated from My love."

   - All have sinned and are not good enough for God's glory (Romans 3:23 NCV).

   - We've compiled this long and sorry record as sinners... and proved that we are utterly incapable of living the glorious lives God wills for us (Romans 3:23 MSG).

   - And when a person knows the right thing to do but does not do it, then he is sinning (James 4:17 ICB).

   - It is your evil that has separated you from your God. Your sins cause him to turn away from you (Isaiah 59:2 NCV).

"I love you, so I, who am perfect, restored our relationship by paying the penalty for your imperfection."

- But Christ died for us while we were still sinners. In this way God shows his great love for us. We have been made right with God by the blood of Christ's death. So through Christ we will surely be saved from God's anger. I mean that while we were God's enemies, God made friends with us through the death of his Son. Surely, now that we are God's friends, God will save us through his Son's life (Romans 5:8-10 ICB).

- Christ had no sin. But God made him become sin. God did this for us so that in Christ we could become right with God (2 Corinthians 5:21 ICB).

- Christ himself died for you. And that one death paid for your sins. He was not guilty, but he died for those who are guilty. He did this to bring you all to God (1 Peter 3:18 ICB).

- The greatest love a person can show is to die for his friends (John 15:13 NCV).

"To initiate this new relationship, all you need to do is to accept My payment for your imperfection. I cannot make you love Me; that is your choice."

- I mean that you have been saved by grace because you believe. You did not save yourselves. It was a gift from God. You cannot brag that you are saved by the work you have done. God has made us what we are. In Christ Jesus, God made us new people (Ephesians 2:8-10 ICB).

- If you use your mouth to say, "Jesus is Lord," and if you believe in your heart that God raised Jesus from death, then you will be saved (Romans 10:9 ICB).

- And this is eternal life: that men can know you, the only true God, and that men can know Jesus Christ, the One you sent (John 17:3 ICB).

To accept God's love for you, talk to Him and tell Him that you do. Let Him lead the decision-making part of your life. This is a sample prayer:

> Jesus, I am sorry I have chosen to live apart from You. I want You in my life. I accept the payment of love You gave for me by Your death on the cross. Thank You for being my best friend and my God.

2. Attend a local church each week. To discover a strong, healthy church in your area, look up a local Christian bookstore in the yellow pages. Ask the people working there for recommendations.

3. Attend a small group with other parents and explore how the Bible applies to parenthood. (This book is a good one to use for a small group discussion. Questions for discussion are in the back.)

4. Establish a daily devotional time. You may prefer to do this together as a married couple, or you may prefer to learn individually and then share with each other what you have learned. You can study as a family using resources like *Daily Devotions for Kids* or *Family Walk* magazine. If you decide to have family devotions (which we highly recommend), keep in mind this rule of thumb: Your devotional time will be most effective if you keep it to one minute for every year of the age of the youngest child. So if you have children ages two, seven, and nine, plan a two-minute devotion that consists of a Bible verse, a song, and a short prayer.

5. Pray for your children. We pray for ours at breakfast or in the car as we drop them off to school. We pray again at dinner. At the end of the day, we pray for them once more as we send them off to bed (even when they become teens!).

6. Serve God together as a family: Teach a children's Sunday school class, work in the church nursery, volunteer in a soup kitchen, or go on a missions trip. Get involved in the community by serving at school or other volunteer organizations. Find a way to share Jesus as a family.

EIGHT

Decide to Build a Network
A Plan for You and Your Prodigal or Child in Pain

❧❧❧

Our friends Mick and Debi shared a unique idea to motivate teens and young adults to stay on track. It has rescued many hearts on the verge of rebellion.

> When our kids were young and our funds were low, we heard of a pastor in like circumstances. He had a young teenage son who wanted a guitar more than anything. The guitar cost $600, a sum beyond what the father felt he could afford.
>
> Late one night the father received a call from a couple in the church. Their son had gotten into trouble, and the family asked the pastor to come be with them at the police station. Hours later, as the pastor watched the parents lay down a hefty sum to bail their son out of jail and bring him home, he couldn't help but think of his own son and the guitar he wanted.

The next day, the pastor and his son made a trip to the music store and purchased the guitar. As the pastor gave the guitar to his son, he thanked him for making wise choices in his life. The pastor explained that he bought the guitar with "bail money." The implication was clear: The bail was spent, so if the son got in trouble, he would be on his own!

Sometimes, however, despite your best efforts, things don't turn out the way you hoped. The great risk of parenthood is that you may receive an assignment you would never sign up for. We all enter parenting with great expectations and hope for the future. We anticipate our kids will be healthy, strong, and productive. But what if that's not the way things work out? What if one of these experiences forever changes the landscape of your family and challenges you to the core of your heart?

- You receive a call in the middle of the night...
- The doctor says, "I'm afraid..."
- A police officer shows up at your door...
- Your child says...

  I'm pregnant.

  I'm gay.

  I'm living with my boyfriend.

  I don't believe in God.

- You've tried everything to help your child heal, and you're told, "This is as good as it gets."

Parenting can feel so overwhelming and heartbreaking that at times you feel as if you want out! You have no one to pass the buck to, and you can't seem to get a break, so you contemplate quitting.

Obviously, this is not an option. Situations like these irreversibly change our lives. We are forced to redefine who we are, how we live, how we manage our time, and how we prioritize our expenses. In a word, we must become selfless. God evidently thinks you can handle the circumstances you're in; He knows that somehow you have what it takes to love this child. You are part of a privileged class even though you may feel as if you are being punished.

Two situations can especially hinder you from finding the treasure God has placed in your child. One is the child with special needs, and the other is the child who has buried the treasure within by becoming a prodigal and running from God. In both cases, the treasure hides under a thick cover of challenges and questions. You want to rescue your child, but you can't do it alone. So instead of losing heart and giving up, decide now to build a network for you and your child.

Choose to Network with God

It may be hard to hear, but the truth is that God will somehow, someway, at some time bring good out of your situation. He is a redeemer who takes the broken parts of our lives and turns them into something better. Your life is going to be a miracle of His grace. That is the intent of Romans 8:28: "And we know that in all things God works for the good of those who love him, who have been called according to his purpose." In a way that is often unexplainable in human terms, God weaves the positive parts of our lives together with the horrendous parts of our lives to bring about good. Most of us probably wish God intervened to prohibit bad things from happening, but that is obviously not how He works. Instead, He allows a strenuous mixture of events to shape us and accomplish His will. The purpose is to make us selfless. He knows that apart from Him we can do nothing of lasting value, so He works in the midst of life to help us get over ourselves. This is God's goal for all parents, but if your journey in parenthood has led you down a particularly difficult path, you will learn selflessness at a much deeper level. Admittedly, this is hard to accept but extremely valuable.

In the movie *Indiana Jones and the Last Crusade,* the main character endures all kinds of frightening episodes on his way to find the treasure: an earthquake, snakes, spiders, robbers, obstacles of every shape and size. Finally, he must step off a cliff and trust that a bridge will magically appear to carry him to safety on the other side. He has to take an unimaginable step of faith. It appears that the step will take him to his own destruction when in reality it is safe and secure.

Is that how you feel? Do you feel as though you have been running a marathon obstacle course, and now God is asking you to step off a cliff into the unknown?

God Is in the Midst of Life's Surprises

Jasmine, whose daughter was pregnant outside of marriage, said, "My daughter relied heavily on me during her crisis because she knew I was in constant contact with God, and she trusted my advice and guidance." Jasmine recommends that you "take every opportunity to grow in the Lord yourself. Feed yourself every day with God's Word through reading and studying the Bible, reading Christian books and magazines, and listening to Christian radio and music."

Find a team who will help you maintain your trust in God. Most of the mothers we surveyed recommended joining a Moms In Touch group. This national organization has groups in most cities representing almost every school. Groups of mothers gather to pray for each school. There are Moms In Touch groups for elementary years through college, and in some cities have a Moms Still in Touch group for mothers of prodigal children who might not even be in school anymore because of their choices.

Listen to Jasmine as she shared her pain in one Moms In Touch group:

> The week before Thanksgiving, Leslie came to me and told me she was pregnant. Unbelievably, I found myself not encouraging her in the way she had been raised, which is pro-life. Rather, I encouraged her in her first initial response, which was to have an abortion out of fear of her dad's wrath. These talks on abortion and making an appointment took place between Monday and Friday of that week. On Friday, I went to my Moms In Touch group. Asking for prayer, I poured out my heart and shared how I was *not* guiding my daughter in the way that I should. I cried with every word.

Another mom in the group shared how she was a mother of an adopted son and what a blessing her child has been to both her and her husband. Another mother of five children poured out her heart about how precious her children have been and how precious is the gift of life. A third mom asked, "Jasmine, if her dad would support Leslie and help her through this crisis, would you be pushing for the abortion?"

In my heart I shouted, "Absolutely not!"

From that Friday morning, God led us down the road of life—step by step, hour by hour, day by day, week by week, month by month. Every Friday at my Moms In Touch group we prayed specific prayers for Leslie. We were experiencing incredible victories every week! By February it was truly becoming a celebration of life, not only for Leslie and me, but for everyone who was watching and praying for us.

Her father and I told Leslie we would support, love, and encourage her through her crisis pregnancy. However, if she chose to keep her baby, she would need to have her own apartment and raise her child on her own. She and her baby would not be able to live in our home. We recognized her time of rebellion was out of God's will and out of order.

Leslie chose to make a plan for an adoption. However, when the first family pulled out in April, she thought perhaps God was saying she should keep her child. She spent a week searching for resources to see if it would be feasible to raise her baby, continue her education, live in her own apartment, and work.

Though she discovered she could make it with the vast amount of resources that are available to single mothers, Leslie came to me after that week and said, "Mom, one thing the government cannot provide for my baby is a dad."

Do not be too fast in giving advice. It is so much better to get to the point when *they* come and talk to *you*. If you don't offer the advice first and furiously, they will eventually ask your opinion.

Leslie turned to God again and realized that His plan for the baby and her was an adoption. Through our Moms In Touch prayers, God was able to bring Leslie's heart and head into one accord. Leslie knew this wasn't the right time in her life to have a baby, but that this baby was meant for another family.

The Lord brought a very special Christ-centered couple to Leslie, and she spent her last trimester building a relationship and creating an extended family with them. Kelly Anne was born on July 20 (my birthday). What an incredible day!

God Is in the Midst of Poor Choices

Renee's daughter suffered from chronic depression. At age 15, she chose to seek affection in a sexual relationship, which resulted in a pregnancy. Renee gathered the two sets of parents to pray. Through tears, they all cried together and asked God to somehow bring good out of this situation.

Though Renee felt like retreating, she courageously obeyed God's call on her own life. She encouraged the other parents, "Don't retreat—serve! Be prepared to help others. Keeping our focus on serving Christ is essential."

Toward the third trimester of her daughter's pregnancy, Renee began to find out about other families in the church who were experiencing a similar heartache. "I would send a card of encouragement with my phone number for the mother. I began volunteering at the local crisis pregnancy care clinic. I became the liaison for our church where we 'adopted' an unwed teen mom-to-be and encouraged her and her mother through the pregnancy." Renee's daughter, Pam, had a short turnaround, during which time she married the baby's father. He was a strong Christian young man, and they moved into an apartment owned by Renee and her husband. The couple stabilized, and Pam discovered she was pregnant again. Unfortunately, after the second baby was born, Pam abandoned her husband and children.

As Renee was praying about what to do in response to her daughter's decision, an agonizing request rose up in her heart. She tried to deny it, but she knew that God was asking her to invite her son-in-law to live with her and her husband so he could raise the kids. In the midst of her personal disappointment, God asked her to serve with the simple promise that "My grace will be sufficient for you." Renee's son-in-law has proved to be a good, caring father who is finishing his education so he can provide for his family effectively for the rest of his life.

Renee's determination to stay strong in her own walk with God helped her gain a broader perspective of all the circumstances that have taken place. For years, Renee prayed that God would bring her husband to know Christ, but she never dreamed the answer would come this way. The trauma of having a daughter in crisis opened up her husband's heart. He realized the only way he and the rest of his family would survive would be to lean on God's strength and power, not his own. With firm resolve in the midst of their disappointment, he began a personal relationship with Christ.

> My husband is transformed! My marriage is transformed for the better! What Satan meant for evil, God meant for good. All the prayers aren't answered for my daughter yet, but I am confident that God continues to work His plan for our family, and that plan will bring us a future and a hope.

Renee credits prayer with friends for her ability to hang in there. Meeting each week with Moms In Touch gave her focus. It kept her eyes on Jesus and provided...

- *Direction.* The group encouraged her to seek God always.
- *Support.* They prayed for Renee and Pam.
- *Hope.* She was reminded that God is faithful to answer the prayers of a righteous woman.
- *Strength.* Knowing she can call on others to join her anytime is a real comfort. It is like a triple-braided cord. Their prayers give strength to her own.

God Is in the Midst of Unfair Situations

Lana is another parent who has found necessary strength in her connection to God. Both her sons had medical problems that kept them from bonding with her as small children. As a result, she and her husband have had a long journey parenting special-needs children. In addition, both her sons became prodigals for a period. In the midst of devastating disappointment, she found strength to persevere.

The biggest thing is having a heavenly perspective, trying to see what God is seeing, rather than my earthly perspective. God has shown this perspective primarily through the Word. When I took my eyes off Him, I used to dread getting up. Every day seemed to be a battle. It began as survival. I was in the Word just to survive each day. It has grown in heavenly perspective to a place where I am now willing to endure the fellowship of Christ's sufferings in order to bring the greater glory of God. For example, if God will get the greater glory by me waiting one, two, three, or more years before solving the problem, I am now willing to wait.

Strength came from having a Scripture passage to meditate on. With that passage in mind, I pray, "God give me your heavenly perspective." My world has grown to be more God-centered and less self-centered. It's been a long journey. When you are under ongoing pressure, God does a deeper work. Diamonds are made under pressure. I like the person I am becoming despite the stresses of the situation with my sons.

One of her children has recovered to the point that he is now on the mission field. The other one is on his way back in a recovery center. Here is Lana's advice to parents of wayward kids:

The natural situation isolates because of shame or embarrassment, but the biblical mandate is fellowship. It's natural to want to reject or run away, but God asks us to *embrace* the pain. Naturally I want to become angry or frustrated because of the lack of control, but biblically, God asks me to be a channel of love and forgiveness.

Don't isolate! You need to find other people who have walked the path before you. Whatever the struggle is doesn't matter. You just need parents who have been there. Even some secular groups that have expertise can be helpful. Look for people in successful programs and look early on, before you might need that program.

When you come to a closed door, but you think help for your child is waiting on the other side, trust God and keep knocking. God is a good God, and He doesn't want you locked out of the resources you need for your child. If you feel you don't have the money, He'll get you the resources. If you feel emotionally drained, He'll provide for your child despite your energy level—your network will drag or carry you along. God will connect you. But you have to be open and honest. Get into a network that might know what to do with the information you are sharing.

Every parent we interviewed said praying God's Word was the strongest source of encouragement, strength, and direction for them and their children during these rough seasons.

Network with Others Who Have Walked the Path

You know as well as we do that these strenuous journeys don't have simple solutions. The pain is persistent and the effects go on and on. Often, what is most helpful is simply knowing you are not the only one who has been asked to tackle this kind of challenge. Somehow in the human experience, it helps to hear other people's stories.

I (Pam) had the great fortune to meet a truly amazing mother named Cricket. (With a name like Cricket, she was destined to make a mark in this world!) Her son, Matthew, was born severely disabled, but Cricket decided that every day she would look for God's special blessing. It might be a small thing: a smile, a new movement, something that would say to her heart, "Matthew matters." She tenaciously journaled her feelings, his medical diagnosis, medications, advice, and resources. In all those pages and pages of text, one story rises above the rest. The day Matthew did what no one else in the world could do.

> A young man named Justin has been attending our church for several months. He has always been extremely stand-offish with everyone. Many of the students in the youth group have made efforts to get him involved and be his friend, but he pretty much has nothing to do with anyone. He often is by himself, not interested in anyone else at all. The youth pastor and the adult team workers have all tried unsuccessfully to get him to do anything besides show up.

Justin's appearance is somewhat intimidating and scary. He tends to dress all in black. His hair is shoulder length and usually greasy looking. He always has dog chains all over his body, around his neck, and hanging off his clothes, attached in a variety of places. This makes him a challenge to approach.

> Well, Matthew was linked up with Michael, one of the teen buddies I arranged to accompany my son as he mainstreamed into the youth group. The two of them were sitting in the back row together, Michael in a chair and Matthew in his wheelchair next to him. Justin was standing several feet away, off by himself. Matthew suddenly wanted something out of his backpack, which was hanging on the back of his chair. I helped unzip the bag and then walked away, allowing a more natural procession to happen. Matthew asked Michael to get his snack. Michael looked at me for direction, and I signaled for him to tell Matthew no. Michael signed no to Matthew.
>
> Impulsively, Matthew wheeled himself over to Justin, grabbed his hand and pulled him to the back row. Then Matthew manipulated Justin's hand into the backpack and showed him that Matthew wanted Justin to search for something! Justin found the snack, and the rest was unbelievable. Matthew had Justin help him eat his entire snack. Matthew sat between two young men, holding on to Michael's hand with his left hand and letting Justin feed him on the right.
>
> A couple of times Michael explained to Justin that Matthew really could feed himself. He told Justin that if he held the container, Matthew would get the snack himself. It was the first time any of us have seen Justin interact with *anyone* or say anything to *anyone*. I encouraged him and thanked him repeatedly and attempted to make him feel very special.
>
> In the middle of the encounter, I walked over to the youth pastor and said, "Don't look now, but a miracle is happening. It's the unlikely who will reach the unlikely."
>
> A few weeks later, I asked Justin if he would consider being a buddy to Matthew while he played Challenge Little League. We offered to pick Justin up, drive him home, and

pay him for his time. The two became baseball buddies—on and off the field.

Matthew reached a soul that no pastor, parent, or peer could reach. Often special-needs children change the world by changing us. He is a living example of Psalm 139:14-16, "I praise you because I am fearfully and wonderfully made...your eyes saw my unformed body. All the days ordained for me were written in your book before one of them came to be." He is a reminder that everyone can have an eternal impact because of who God is.

Help to Make It Through the Night

Another mom asked her group of friends to pray for her distraught, depressed teenage son as she and her husband made the heart-wrenching choice to institutionalize him to save his life.

> Our son was hospitalized for a 24-hour observation. He was now an adult, and the facility was quite different from the youth hospital he had been in before for severe depression and a suicide attempt. Once admitted, he could do nothing to be released for 24 hours. He was no longer a minor, so my husband and I couldn't do anything either. He clearly did not want to stay. As I forced a meeting with a supervisor, I caught a glimpse of the large ward where he would stay the night. Men and women of all ages in various states of mental health were all in one room. Our departure was more than difficult as we left our child against our wishes, and his, in this place.
>
> We drove home in silent, tearful prayer. When I arrived home I went straight into my room, knowing that I had the power to send legions of angels to stand guard over my child in that hospital. I knelt by my bed, opened my Bible, and prayed through the night. As long as my child was in that place I would stay awake and pray God's protection over him. I asked God to prompt me in prayer. I asked, "Tell me what he needs right now." At approximately 10:30 PM I felt a deep sense that I needed to pray that God would put a shield all around him—not just any shield but the shield of

righteousness. Total protection. All the armor of Ephesians 6—head to toe coverage! I pled with God to provide safety. As the night wore on, the sense of urgency subsided. But I still had no peace, so I shifted my prayers toward other important requests on his behalf.

We arrived at the hospital one hour ahead of schedule to make sure the paperwork was processed and he could be discharged the moment the doctor gave him the release. When he was released, he told me that this facility was nothing like the youth hospital he had been in before. The experience was frightening. For the first few hours he had begged the nurses on duty to let him go home. One particular nurse pulled him aside saying, "Listen, I know you don't need to be here. You're fine. Stay quiet—it will be all right." At about 10:30 PM she took him inside the nurse's glass-walled station and set up a cot for him for the rest of the night. The glass went from floor to ceiling with a door and a window to the ward. The nurse sat directly next to him as a shield of protection for my son.

Realistic Expectations

Norm Wright is a counselor, influential Christian leader, and author of more than 70 books. He is also the parent of a special-needs child who impacted every decision he and his wife made during their parenting years. He points out that we ought to be careful not to overstate the intent of Proverbs 22:6, which says: "Train a child in the way he should go, and when he is old he will not turn from it."

Some people claim this verse as some kind of inalienable right, as if we can tell God, "You owe me! I trained my child; now give me a godly, productive, successful kid!"

But that's not what it means. Norm offers this explanation in his book *Loving a Prodigal:*

> The proverbs were never intended to be absolute promises from God. Instead, they are probabilities of things likely to occur. The primary author of Proverbs was Solomon, the wisest man on earth at that time. His purpose was to convey

his divinely inspired observations on the way human nature and God's universe work. He was saying that a given set of circumstances can generally be expected to produce a certain set of consequences.[1]

Dr. Gleason Archer sets up realistic parental expectations.

[Parenting means] impressing on [children] that they are very important persons in their own right because they are loved by God and because He has a wonderful and perfect plan for their lives. Parents who have faithfully followed these principles and practices in rearing their children may safely entrust them as adults to the keeping and guidance of God and feel no sense of personal guilt if a child later veers off course. They have done their best before God. The rest is up to each child himself.[2]

Louise Tucker Jones, mother of a Down syndrome son, and coauthor Cheri Fuller, give words of wisdom in *Extraordinary Kids: Nurturing and Championing Your Child with Special Needs.*

- Be kind to yourself. Give yourself time to adjust. Let the other spouse have the freedom to not be where you are emotionally. Pamper yourself when stress hits.

- Pray for yourself and for wisdom to lead your child in the right path and not block God's plan for your child.

- Don't feel as if you have to explain everything to everyone.

- Don't look too far forward or too far backward. Concentrate on today.

- Be honest with your feelings.

- You have lost an expectation, but you have gained a child.

- Lay any negative diagnosis at [Jesus'] feet, and listen for His direction.

- Don't let fear of a disability, an illness, or the future rule your life. God is sovereign![3]

Network with Supportive Friends

Arrianne was beaten by her husband, as were her children. Finally, after her husband had physically abused her 11-year-old son, she gathered the courage to call for help. The pain from years of abuse and the subsequent divorce sent Arrianne's son, Curt, over the edge. He looked for dramatic ways to numb the pain. He turned to alcohol, drugs, and girls. One day, the high school called because Curt was violently ill. Doctors discovered he was addicted to marijuana, acid, prescription pain killers, and crystal methamphetamine. The news was devastating for Arrianne as a flood of reactions crashed upon her. "I knew my son was hurting, but I didn't realize it was this bad. What have I done wrong? Why couldn't I stop this? Does he know I love him? What can I do to help? What should I do?" She was instantly overwhelmed, and even Curt's rebellious attitude gave way to fear when he was tested for HIV.

> I didn't feel alone, even though I easily could have. Our church has the habit of placing a support group around people who have a family crisis. I had one since the day I first called for help a few years before. So when we got this devastating news, I called my support team.

The team was there when she had to weigh out decisions to call 911 to protect herself and her other children from Curt's violent temper. The group was there as he entered various treatment programs, broke the law, and entered juvenile hall. The team stood by her side when she convinced officials to test Curt for mental illness, and they continued to stand by when she received various reports. The support team stuck by her when he ran away numerous times from treatment facilities. The team encouraged her to step out and find a better job. They helped her gain perspective on the problems with Curt's siblings. They backed her up as Curt wrapped up his treatment program, was released from jail, and began his probation. The team rejoiced with her as Curt transitioned into being a productive citizen who completed a GED and secured a job.

My support team helped me take each step. For me, talking through a situation, expressing my feelings, and getting sound advice from people who knew the scoop helped me put my feelings and ideas into action. I shared the ugliness, fears, and doubts that would overwhelm some people. My support team's commitment to me and my family made life doable. God remade my instincts. Where before I was paralyzed by fear, I learned to instinctively cry out to God at the first call with bad news. Next I would call my support team, who prayed as I made the next call or decision. Sometimes they just listened, and God turned my panic into His peace.

Arrianne gives this advice to moms of kids in pain and prodigals:

Know you are not alone. There are many more moms in pain than any of us want to admit. Making that first desperate call for help is hard. You may not want people to see what your life is like, but when you let people in, change happens. From that point on, you will never want to go back to the way your life was before because you have grown. Yes, life can be depressing and very overwhelming at times, but when you go one day at a time (or sometimes one hour or one minute!), you find a way to get through. Just doing the next normal thing, like getting dressed or making dinner, can seem like a huge step. Knowing you have friends walking alongside helps move you forward.

Build a Network for Your Child

Jan never dreamed she would be the mom of a promiscuous, suicidal teen, but that is exactly what Jordan became. You can hear the distress in Jan's words, "It felt like I was watching her die slowly, and nothing I could say or do seemed to matter. She even told me, 'Mom, you can't save me, so stop trying.'"

Of course, Jan didn't stop trying. She never gave up on her daughter or the promise that "He who began a good work in Jordan will be faithful to complete it" (Philippians 1:6, paraphrased). Jan said others were better at reaching Jordan's heart than she was at times.

> The greatest source of strength came from friends of mine who loved Jordan without judging her. I desperately needed to hear others say that they believed in her. The godly mentors who were in place at the time Jordan took her detour turned out to make the biggest difference. They were friends of hers and mine who cared about her and continued to keep in contact with her. At first this was hard for me. It felt as if she trusted them more than me and was confiding only in them. But as time went on, I realized that God had provided these friends to love her through a very difficult time.

Later, Jordan shared that there are times in prodigals' lives when they aren't ready to come back. They want control of their lives and choices, but they are feeling God draw them back. Confiding in their parents would risk too much of the control, or they might feel they would hurt or disappoint their parents more. The friends served as a kind of testing ground or oasis on their journey home. Jan recounts one critical time:

> There was a time when Jordan felt so hopeless she actually planned out her own suicide. It was to be on a Monday. The weekend prior to that Monday, our church youth group was going on a weekend retreat. To my surprise, Jordan wanted to go. I prayed continually the entire weekend that something she heard would change her life. She called me the first evening to say she was bored. My heart sank, but I continued to pray. The next day Jordan felt God was leading her forward during the altar call to rededicate her life to Christ. She might not have had the courage, but Rochelle, one of those godly mentors, was there to walk with her.

Give Yourself Permission to Grieve

You may feel devastated when your child alters your life forever. The dream you had for your family gets swallowed up. Disappointment overshadows your hopes. The atmosphere of encouragement and growth you set out to create withers under the constant demands of your child's choices. You will experience grief as you would with any loss, and it may include these feelings:

- *Denial.* I can't believe this is happening to me.
- *Anxiety.* How can I possibly handle this?
- *Fear.* What will happen to my child and my family?
- *Guilt.* What did I do to cause this?
- *Depression.* My hopes and dreams seem lost forever.
- *Anger.* This isn't fair.
- *Acceptance.* I don't like what has happened. I don't understand why it happened. I don't know how I'm going to handle this. But God knows, and I can trust Him.[4]

The key is to give yourself permission to grieve. When God created Adam and Eve, He designed them to live forever. Their kids were going to live forever, and they were all going to make good decisions. But they chose to disobey God, and loss became a part of the human experience. Because it is unnatural, it is hard. Every loss, whether big or small, creates emotional turmoil within you. Every stage of grief helps your system release the emotional confusion that builds up. The intensity of the emotions is an expression of your love for your child. Martha Little, mother of a child with special needs, offers the following steps to acceptance:

- *Acknowledge* that God's hand was on your children before birth and formed them according to His plan.
- *Admit* any areas you resent in the way God made them.
- *Accept* God's design for them. Thank Him for their personalities and the way they are.
- *Affirm* God's purpose in creating them for His glory.
- *Ally* yourself with God in His plans for them.[5]

Decision Point
Build a Network

When the crises hit in your family, do not go through the parenting challenge alone! Check the list below and choose the next step in building your network of helpful people and resources:

Get Emergency Help

Some cases, like trouble with the law, a suicide attempt, expulsion from school, or a teen pregnancy, need immediate care. If your son or daughter suffered physical trauma, you'd take them to an emergency room, right? In the same way, most families in crisis need a short-term plan to deal with the issues at hand. A qualified pastor, Christian counselor, or youth leader might be a good first phone call. They will most likely know referrals for your other needs (legal aid, emotional help, schooling, and homes for teens in trouble).

Create a Long-Term Plan

- *Get help for you and your spouse.* If parents feel supported, understood, and strengthened, they make better choices with and for their prodigal. Seek to maintain a united front by making decisions together. Prodigals may try to use guilt or manipulation to get one of you to cave in and endorse or subsidize their unhealthy behavior. Use your time in the counseling office to create a unified plan that you both feel you can realistically carry out.

- *Get help for your prodigal.* If they are not willing, use this time to investigate options for when they do become willing. But if they are willing...

- *Go for something over nothing.* This means that even if they won't repent or acknowledge that their choices are wrong or unhealthy, ask if they are willing to meet with a pastor, a counselor, or a trusted friend—someone who might break through to them or at least be a part of their team when they do decide to come around.

- *Try to keep contact.* It is hard to help if you don't know how to reach them. This isn't always possible, but at least keep your same phone number, e-mail, and home in case they want to contact you. (If this goes on for years, your support team will be a good sounding board for you should you need to relocate your family.)

- *Find something positive to build on.* Look for something they *are* doing right. It might take prayer and creativity to discern something, but look for one positive thing and start building on it to rebuild the relationship. This is often the cord they use to pull themselves back into God's (and your) good graces. It gives them a foundation, something firm to stand on when everything in their life seems unstable.

- *Decide what to say and who needs to know about your prodigal's choices.* Decide ahead of time how you will handle questions and unsolicited advice.

- *Stabilize your family.* Get a plan together to provide the best care and help for the children who remain in your home and are not prodigals. If you spend all your time on the prodigal, the other children will feel neglected, and you may end up with a repeat performance. Look for ways to bless and encourage the prodigal's siblings. Try to normalize family life as best as you can.

Never Give Up Hope

Regardless of what has happened, never stop asking God to pursue your children. Sandy, who had a drug-using runaway son, prayed, "God, run him down to get him the help he needs." That day the pastor of his church almost hit him with his car as the boy darted across traffic! The pastor recognized him and took him to breakfast. He then called Sandy so she'd know her son was all right. Without another word, everyone involved knew that God was watching out for him!

NINE

Decide to Trust
Transferring the Treasure to Your Teen

∾∾∾

Will they try drugs? Is she going to get pregnant? Is he going to get in a fight? Are they drinking and driving? This world can fill our hearts and lives with so much fear that we might want to never let our children out of our house or out of our sight! However, if we overprotect our children in their teen years, we cripple them and their development, and we may never see the thing we most want—a responsible, moral, independent adult child. We can become our own worst enemy. Fear can drive us parents to create crazy rules like these:

Rules for Dating My Daughter

Rule one: If you pull into my driveway and honk, you'd better be delivering a package, because you're sure not picking anything up.

Rule two: You do not touch my daughter in front of me. You may glance at her as long as you do not peer at anything below her neck.

If you cannot keep your eyes or hands off of my daughter's body, I will remove them.

Rule three: I am aware that it is considered fashionable for boys of your age to wear their trousers so loosely that they appear to be falling off their hips. I want to be fair and open-minded about this issue, so I propose this compromise: You may come to the door with your underwear showing and your pants ten sizes too big, and I will not object. However, in order to ensure that your clothes do not, in fact, come off during the course of your date with my daughter, I will take my electric nail gun and fasten your trousers securely in place to your waist.

Rule four: It is usually understood that in order for us to get to know each other, we should talk about sports, politics, and other issues of the day. Please do not do this. The only information I require from you is an indication of when you expect to have my daughter safely back at my house, and the only word I need from you on this subject is *early*.

Rule five: I'm sure you've been told that in today's world, promiscuity can kill you. Let me elaborate: If you are promiscuous with my daughter, I will kill you.

Rule six: I have no doubt you are a popular fellow with many opportunities to date other girls. This is fine with me as long as it is okay with my daughter. If you make her cry, I will make you cry.

Rule seven: As you stand in my front hallway, waiting for my daughter to appear, and more than an hour goes by, do not sigh and fidget. If you want to be on time for the movie, you should not be dating. Instead of just standing there, why don't you do something useful like changing the oil in my car?

Rule eight: The following places are not appropriate for a date with my daughter: Places where there are beds, sofas, or anything softer than a wooden stool. Places where there are no parents, policemen, or nuns within eyesight. Places where there is darkness. Places where there is dancing, holding hands, or happiness. Places where the ambient temperature is warm enough to induce my daughter to wear shorts, tank tops, midriff T-shirts, or anything other than overalls, a sweater, and a goose down parka zipped up to her throat. Movies with a strong romantic or sexual theme are to be avoided; movies that feature chain saws are okay. Hockey games are okay. Old folks' homes are better.

Rule nine: Do not lie to me. I may appear to be a potbellied, balding, middle-aged, dimwitted has-been. But on issues relating to my daughter, I am the all-knowing, merciless god of your universe. If I ask you where you are going and with whom, you have one chance to tell me the truth, the whole truth, and nothing but the truth. I have a shotgun, a shovel, and five acres behind the house. Do not trifle with me.

Rule ten: Be afraid. Be very afraid. It takes very little for me to mistake the sound of your car in the driveway for a chopper coming in over a rice paddy outside of Hanoi. When my reaction to Agent Orange starts acting up, the voices in my head frequently tell me to clean the guns as I wait for you to bring my daughter home. As soon as you pull into the driveway you should exit your car with both hands in plain sight. Speak the perimeter password, announce in a clear voice that you have brought my daughter home safely and early, and return to your car—there is no need for you to come inside. The camouflaged face at the window is mine.

An overreaction? Of course. However, too often our fears as parents drive us to overreact. There are two ways to parent a teen: by fear or by faith. *Decide to trust.* Methodically transfer responsibility from your plate to your teens' as they move toward adulthood. When you decide to trust yourself and your teen and you have a plan in place to entrust to them all they need to succeed, your fears will subside.

The Big Picture

Communicate to your kids that God has a plan to bless their future as they prepare to receive the precious things God wants to entrust to them: complete responsibility for their own lives and futures. *If you honor God, God will honor you.* That is a phrase our children have heard over and over and over again since they were small. The Bible is full of examples.

Moses refused to be called Pharaoh's son and instead chose to identify himself with the people of God. After a short stint at the backside of a desert shepherding sheep, he led his people out of captivity and now lives in history.

Daniel refused the king's food and instead chose to eat according to God's laws. Daniel also refused to bow to an idol and was thrown in a lions' den, only to be miraculously saved and elevated by God to leadership of the world's most powerful nation of the time.

Shadrach, Meshach, and Abednego refused to bow and worship the king because they worshiped God. They were thrown into a fiery furnace and saved from it. They were visited there by the angel of God, which many theologians believe to be Jesus Christ.

God told Samuel to anoint a boy as king, and when Samuel questioned God, He said, "Man looks at the outward appearance, but the LORD looks at the heart" (1 Samuel 16:7). David, a shepherd known as a man after God's own heart, became king of Israel.

Consider theses verses:

- No good thing does He withhold from those who walk uprightly (Psalm 84:11 NASB).

- My shield is God Most High, who saves the upright in heart (Psalm 7:10).

- Blessed is the man who fears the LORD, who finds great delight in his commands. His children will be mighty in the land; the generation of the upright will be blessed (Psalm 112:1-2).

- In my integrity you uphold me and set me in your presence forever (Psalm 41:12).

- Righteousness guards the man of integrity (Proverbs 13:6).

- Trust in the LORD with all your heart and lean not on your own understanding; in all your ways acknowledge him, and he will make your paths straight (Proverbs 3:5-6).

- His master replied, "Well done, good and faithful servant! You have been faithful with a few things; I will put you in charge of many things. Come and share your master's happiness!" (Matthew 25:23).

- Those who honor me I will honor (1 Samuel 2:30).

If our kids didn't get anything else from us during their growing-up years, we pray they got this sweeping principle: *Those who honor God, God honors.* All it takes is a humble heart. First Peter 5:6 explains, "Humble yourselves, therefore, under God's mighty hand, that he may lift you up in due time."

Teen Means Transition

We believe a person's basic character is set by age 12. You might be able to do a little training and teaching in the junior high years, but character flaws are very difficult to correct after sixth grade and even harder in high school. Junior highers can learn volumes of information; however, their moral character is pretty much in place. Yes, God can always do an amazing, transforming work in any person's life at any age, but it is just that—work, and a work that God has to orchestrate and implement.

If you have parented well before your kids turn 13, their teen years will be an exciting delight as you watch the fruit of your labors unfold before your very eyes. You have most likely picked up by now a couple of key parental guidelines we strove to place in our children early:

- Integrity is not optional. A good name is the best asset you have.

- Servant hearts will be rewarded. People respond to servant leadership.

- Never expect others to do what you are unwilling to do.

- You can't please everyone, so strive to please God. If you please Him, you will most likely also be pleasing those who are godly.

- A positive attitude won't get you everything, but it will get you a whole lot more than a negative attitude will.

- Speak with a respectful attitude. You don't have to agree with us, but you do have to honor us as your parents.

As your kids enter the teen years, your parenting styles will change. For the first 12 years of your child's life, you set the boundaries and decided the rules, schedules, and priorities. However, now that your child is a teen, your job as a parent has changed. Your role now is to systematically, little by little, transfer responsibility to your teens so that by the time they are adults, they are fully responsible for their own lives.

We often hear parents complain that their 30-year-old still lives at home, or that their young adult daughter keeps dating losers, or that their son can't keep a job. Many times you can trace these kinds of adult stresses back to their parents' inability to hand the reins over to the child.

If you keep being a directive parent (a benevolent dictator), then in your kids' teen years they will feel that they have to wrestle the reins of their lives away from you. If you are fortunate, your teens will speak out. But this isn't always done in a very respectful manner. If you have consistently dictated to them, they may not feel that you will hear them, so they may yell or say ugly things to try to get your attention.

When this very common form of declaring independence happened at our home, we'd simply and unemotionally remind our teens that they could express most any feeling if they did it with respectful words and in a respectful tone. When they failed to communicate respectfully, we would say, "Want to try that again?"

When It Gets Worse

Other times, teens will assert their independence through acts of rebellion. They just will not do as you have asked. The most dangerous tactics are manipulation and lying—the teen tells you what you want to hear and then does just the opposite when you are not around. This can go undetected for months or even years if your child is a good liar.

In our diligence to encourage children toward excellence, we sometimes unknowingly (or knowingly) replace inner conscience and conviction with outer rules and legalism. This puts teens in a double bind. They don't want to hurt their parents, but the narrow restrictions simply do not work in the real world. Some teens choose passive-aggressive behaviors of acting one way at home and church, and then living differently elsewhere. Your daughter might walk out the door wearing a floral mid-calf dress but hiding a miniskirt in her purse. Your son might say "Yes, sir" and "Yes, ma'am" and then walk right out and do the opposite of what you have asked.

Other parents abdicate their duties during their kids' teen years. Some parents expect their 14-year-olds to find all their own rides to and from school, sports, and activities, work to pay for all their own needs, and maybe help out the family too. Some teens feel that they are parenting not only themselves, but their siblings and often their own parents as well.

Sometimes, teens take this abdication in stride and simply decide that when they have families of their own, they will try to be more responsible. Other teens merely delay their rebellion. They are responsible through young adulthood and perhaps until their younger siblings are out of the home. Then they decide to experience all the fun they missed. Unfortunately, by this time they could be married and even have children of their own.

Most of the time, however, teens of disengaged parents follow their parents' example and refuse to grow up. This is one reason why alcoholism, drug abuse, and teen pregnancy often repeat generation after generation. Most people would rather endure familiar patterns of pain than to embrace the unfamiliar process of change required to develop healthier lives.

Because you care enough to be reading this book, you are not likely to dump your duties as a parent. On the other hand, even though you may have the best of intentions, you may be tempted to reign in your kids too tightly. If you do, your kids may not be prepared for the freedom they will one day face, and they may give in to the temptations you so diligently protected from.

Several of our friends grew up on the mission field. One of them told us about her best friend. Both girls had parents who were missionaries, but my friend's parents gave her room to grow. They encouraged her to express her opinions as long as she did it respectfully, and they asked her to think through her own decisions. Her friend, however, was not allowed to ever disagree with her parents. She was not allowed to wear makeup, dress in fashions from the States, or ever be alone with a boy for any reason. She wasn't allowed to think independently. When she went away to Bible college, her parents were shocked to discover she was on probation because she hadn't gone to class, was living off campus with a divorced man who was 15 years her senior, and was pregnant. "How could this happen to our perfect little girl?"

It happened partly because she was never given responsibility for her own life. She never developed her own value system. Kids like this girl can easily become prey to the strongest, most charismatic person around them even if that person's values oppose the kids' parents'—and sometimes *because* those values are the opposite of Mom and Dad's.

Instead of dictating your teens' behavior and forcing your will on them, plan to transfer to them bit by bit the responsibility for their lives. At the end of this chapter you will find several worksheets (contracts) you can give to your teen. This is one way of transferring the major areas of responsibility. These, accompanied with the Learner and Leader contracts, should help you release your teen slowly and carefully into the adult world.

These contracts have their roots in our years in youth ministry. We found our teens needed a tool to give their parents confidence, and the parents needed a tool to help structure the release of responsibility. We tried to encourage parents to let the teens struggle to set up their own value system rather than struggle against Mom and Dad. If you are a dictator, your teens may rebel simply to express their opinions. Teens will often talk out loud, testing their value system.

Teens might say outrageous things, such as "What's wrong with sex outside marriage?" or "What's the big deal about drinking?" or "I'm not sure I believe in God anymore." These statements can shake a parent to the core, and many parents respond by tightening the reins. Unfortunately, tighter reins usually create more outrageous statements, which can lead to outrageous behavior.

On the other hand, if you allow your teens to think through the major areas of their lives (relationships, driving, working, education, social commitments, and faith) and choose their own structure, boundaries, and consequences for violations, you are no longer seen as the bad guy. You simply enforce the consequences your teens have chosen.

This frightens some parents. Many think teens will choose "light sentences," but we have actually experienced the opposite. If you let your preteens choose their own punishment, they will probably be harder on themselves than you might be.

Let's look at an example. When our own kids were growing up, we gave information about sex and relationships on a need-to-know basis. We had three major talks and many other mini discussions with them. In early elementary years (or before if I was pregnant), they learned the basics of where babies come from. Then when they were nine or ten, we explained menstruation and how to treat girls. This talk came just before any of their friends who were girls began menses, so if anything happened to one of their classmates while at school, they were able to handle the situation like gentlemen.

When the boys entered junior high, Bill talked with them about their own changing bodies, lust, wet dreams, masturbation, and so on. Then the summer before they entered high school, Bill gave them some pointers on how to choose a woman well and how to recognize and avoid high-maintenance women. Both of us joined in for a session on why we recommend group dating in high school, and then we assigned several books for them to read to gain the next set of privileges.

Our children have grown up hearing our story of romance. We both came from homes where the marriage wasn't strong or very healthy. My (Pam's) parents eventually divorced. My mother came to fear for our lives because of the violent effect alcohol had on my father. Bill and I wanted to build a love relationship God's way. We decided to wait until he proposed before we kissed because prior to our rededication to Christ, we'd both been in relationships where the people we were dating wanted more sexually than we wanted to give, and we had felt pressure. We maintained our virginity in high school, but we both knew we were wired hot, so the sexual drive was not something to be taken lightly or a game to be played. The day Bill bent on one knee, sang me a song he had written, and proposed was the day we first kissed. We have had, to date, 26 very happy and sexually fulfilling years together.

When our children were in junior high, we began working on a relationship contract worksheet:

1. *Describe the traits of the person you would someday like to marry.* List verses that describe the person God would want your son or daughter to someday marry. People marry the kind of people they date.

2. *How will you know if the person you would like to date has those traits?* Your kids may point to the way their potential dates treat their parents or friends. If your kids say they want to marry a Christian, encourage them to write a more specific description like this: "...a Christian with an active growing faith that would be reflected in church and youth group attendance, service, and a personal devotional time daily."

3. *What is your dating philosophy?* (We recommend reading two or three of these books: *I Kissed Dating Goodbye, I Gave Dating a Chance, 10 Commandments of Dating,* or *Decide in Two Dates or Less.* See your local bookstore.) Will your kids choose to court only someone they are considering marrying, or will they choose to date socially? The key is that both the kids and parents pray through and agree on the philosophy ahead of time. Develop an open dialogue on this topic because the details of the relationship contract may evolve over time.

4. *What is the definition of a date?* Ours is any prearranged time between two people.

5. *How will we know you are responsible enough to...*
   - group date?
   - double date?
   - single date?

6. *What kinds of dates will you go on at what age?* Include a discussion of proms and other special activities.

7. *Write a list of at least ten active dates.* Active dates are those that foster discussion and steer the daters clear of temptation. Passive dates like movies, videos, and just hanging out are setups for a sexual fall.

8. *What are God's physical standards for your relationships at different stages?* We draw a line with holding hands on one end and sexual intercourse on the other, and we have our sons look up a variety of Bible verses and put marks on the line for casual relationships, serious dating headed to courtship, engagement, and marriage.

9. *Who will pay for dates? How will they be paid for?* We don't underwrite our kids' social lives except for youth group events.

10. *Who are two people—one best friend, one adult other than my parents—to whom I can give this contract so they will hold me accountable?* These people will help you guide and guard your precious children as they begin exploring relationships with the opposite sex.

11. *What are the consequences if I break my contract?* Have them list consequences for first, second, and third offenses. This is imperative because it makes them "the heavy," and you will only enforce what they have already set in place as their own consequence.

Add your family traditions to the worksheet. For example, we want to meet anyone whom our sons are interested in dating. No one of the opposite sex is allowed in our sons' rooms when we are home or in our house when we are not home. Also, when our sons think they are ready to solo date, they must meet with the parents of the girl and explain their standards and ask for permission to date their daughter. You might have your own traditions.

Sign and date the document. We encourage you to begin discussing these issues and writing the relationship contract in your kids' preteen years. Most children begin to be interested in the opposite gender in junior high, so this is a great time for you to have them complete the relationship contract. However, it's never too late for the relationship contract—even college-age students will discuss and complete agreements if they are tied to their college tuition check.

We've found the more we talk about these issues ahead of time, the less likely we are to experience conflict and the more likely our children are to make wise choices. The best way to guarantee your children will have happy marriages is to protect them from poor relational choices as teens and young adults, and the relationship contract is one tool to help your kids decide before God that they want healthy, happy relationships and will make good choices to ensure they will have them.

Train and Transfer

We have tried to train our kids step-by-step as they have grown. On the Learner and Leader chore chart, we might have written, "Clean your room," but we knew our version of *clean* and a nine-year-old's would be very different, so we made 3 x 5 cards and a checklist they could follow so they would know what we meant by a clean room. For example:

- Fold clothes and put them away.
- Dust shelves, headboard, desk, and tables.
- Put toys in right bins.
- Organize papers and books so we could find something if you sent me to your room to find it.

We want to set our kids up for success. That's why we tell them, "You can make your own decision as soon as we know you are prepared to make the right decision." This is where the transfer begins.

Pros and Cons

As the kids hit eight, nine, ten, and eleven, we sat down with them when any kind of major decision came and said, "We need to make a decision. Let's make a list of pros and cons for each option and then pray and see how God leads us." We didn't do this for every decision but only when we thought the situation was a good opportunity to learn decision-making skills.

Here is an example: Zach was on an all-star baseball team that had a Sunday game when he was nine. We helped him make a list:

Pros

- He would keep his commitment to the team.
- He could go to the 8:30 church service before the 11:30 game.

- He could take Jesus with him and even offer to pray before the game.
- It is a play-off game. If he is missing, they might lose, and he might have made the difference.
- A parent has already volunteered to pick him up at church and take him so Mom and Dad won't have to miss their responsibilities.
- Mom and Dad can come and see the last half of the game and pick up Zach.
- The non-Christians might see his missing the game as a sign of his religion being legalistic with no flexibility.

Cons
- Some might see this as putting baseball over God.
- Mom and Dad might get tied up after church and only make the last inning or so.
- The family gets fast food and not a nice Sunday lunch.
- Zach will miss children's church (but not Sunday school).
- Mom and Dad can't drive him there. Are Zach and Mom and Dad comfortable with the person who volunteered?

Then we taught the kids to mark each reason as an A, B, or C reason, and we have them compare the As on each list. This way, they compare the top priorities instead of choosing the longest list. Zach decided that this time, because he could still go to church at 8:30 and because he was strategic for a win in a play-off, he would go and not let down the pre-believers on his team we all had been sharing with and inviting to church. We felt comfortable with the parent who volunteered to drive, and our family had been praying theirs would come to faith in Christ and begin attending church.

However, the next fall, Zach made a different choice when a game that was scheduled for Sunday at 1:00 was moved to 10:30. It was a regular game, it was winter ball (so no standings were taken), and he'd have to miss both worship services. Zach called his coach and said, "Coach, Jesus is more important to me than baseball. Because the game got moved to a time when my family attends church and there are no other options for me to attend at a different time, I will miss this week's game. Could you tell the league board that it would be helpful if they kept their word? I signed up because they said all games would be on Sunday after 1:00, and this one isn't, so that means all of us kids have to make a choice to skip church if our families go to church. I don't think that is right. Sorry, Coach. I'll pray you still win." That season, two more games were moved, and Zach missed both of them to attend church. He said it was a matter of principle. After that season, Zach made a decision to never sign up for a league in any sport that played only Sunday games.

Had we laid down the law and just imposed our decision, our son might have rebelled because he didn't understand, and he would have missed out on the foundation that was laid for future decisions.

What Kids Need from Parents at Different Stages

Below is a chart that shows how our parenting changes through the ages and stages of our children's lives.

You and Your Child's Development

Your child's stages of life	Your child's approach to life	Your child's needs	Your role as a parent
Early Childhood Infancy through preschool	**Dependency** Your child needs you in every way imaginable and only knows about the part of the world you introduce him or her to.	**Establish a bond** Your child needs to establish an emotional and social bond with you through physical touch, fair discipline, and playtime.	**Decision maker** You must make most decisions for your child and discern what is best for him or her.
Childhood Kindergarten to puberty	**Exploration** School introduces your child to a big new world. He or she will be fascinated by it and be motivated to explore the possibilities.	**Set goals and find an activity to excel in** The world is a big place, so kids must learn to prioritize and set goals, and to discover a unique ability that will give them confidence now and later.	**Director** Your child needs you to lay out healthy options for exploration and direct him or her to get involved.

Your child's stages of life	Your child's approach to life	Your child's needs	Your role as a parent
Adolescence Puberty to age 18	Experimentation Teenagers discover who they are by experimenting with different identities in different situations. Increased hormonal levels limit their ability to think clearly but intensify their emotional responses to experiences.	Make wise decisions This is a time of turmoil as teenagers try to figure out their place in life. They may avoid accepting responsibility for their decisions. They need to see the long-term effect of their decisions—positive and negative.	Coach Enable your teens to make as many decisions as possible. Coach them into making good decisions while you retain veto power. Ask questions such as, "What do you think we should we do?" or "Tell me why I should say Yes."
Early Adulthood Ages 19 to 30	Application Young adults have established their identity. Now they live out this conclusion by making choices about career, family, and community.	Establish mentoring and encouraging relationships Your children will seek your affirmation and wisdom without compromising their independence.	Consultant Wait to be asked and only intervene when absolutely necessary. Launch your child into an independent life.
Adulthood Ages 30 and over	Interdependence Your children have figured out their place in life and realized that we are on this journey together. They will value others' contributions and will be attracted to supportive relationships.	Establish peer relationships Your children are now your adult peers. Their talents and contributions to life is equal to or greater than yours.	Peer It is now time to be friends. You have a unique place in life and so does your child. You can now contribute to one another's life as equals.

Work Yourself Out of a Job

Your goal as a parent is to work yourself out of the role of overseeing your children's lives and, piece by piece, give that responsibility to them by the time they are 18. There are many ways to do this.

Dave and Claudia Arp, in their book *Suddenly They're 13*, share an idea that you may want to adapt as your own children enter the teen years.

Becoming a teenager at our house was a big deal. After the family celebration, we planned another time to take our new teenager out to dinner with just the two of us. On this special occasion we tried to communicate the following message:

We are excited about your growing up. You are now a teenager, and we want to relate to you on a more adult level. In five short years you will be eighteen and will probably be leaving for college. We want you to be prepared to make your own decisions, run your own life, and function as an adult. So for the next five years on your birthday each year we will give you new and expanded privileges and responsibilities for the coming year. Our goal is that by the time you're eighteen you will achieve adult status—not only physically, but mentally, spiritually, and emotionally as well.[1]

The Arps then presented their teen with a small wooden box filled with 3 x 5 cards. On each card they listed a new privilege or responsibility for the coming year.

In my (Pam's) book *Got Teens?* (coauthored with Jill Savage), I list 11 areas of life that moms need to hand over to their teens by the time the kids are 22. The premise is that God will give us parents what we need to give our teens in key areas like finances, relationships, life skills, and a relationship with God. Our systems may vary, but every parent needs to think through the question, how can we give our teens the reins of life in small steps so they can succeed at running their own lives by their early twenties? We decided we'd aim at preparing our kids to handle adult responsibilities by the time they were 18. We chose this age partly because that's when boys must register with Selective Service. We couldn't determine whether our country would be at war, so we needed to prepare them just in case the very worst case scenario happened and they needed to fight for their lives (and defend ours). Owning responsibility for their lives by 18 was the goal. However, most families add the finishing touches in the college years. We found that if 18 was the goal, we could easily make minor adjustments in the college years.

Tell Me Why I Should Say Yes

As kids move through junior high, they can participate in making decisions by telling you why you should say yes.

James (not his real name) once called Brock and asked if Brock could spend the night and then go to Disneyland the next day with James' grandparents. Brock looked up at us from the phone and asked if he could go. We replied, "Get as much information as possible and tell him you will call him back after you talk to your parents."

When Brock hung up the phone, we said, "Tell us why we should say yes."

Brock had created lists of pros and cons with us for several years, so now he created his own on a piece of paper. He wrote down questions he knew we'd ask and the answers to them.

Pros

- I love Disneyland and haven't gone for a while.
- I can use my own money if Mom and Dad say I need to.
- Mom knows James and likes him.
- James' grandparents will be driving.
- I don't have any commitments on Saturday.
- I can get Saturday's chores done on Thursday.
- I have been responsible in handling my way to and from school. I always call if there is a problem. I know how to ask for help or directions and how to avoid dangerous people. I can navigate Disneyland even if James and I are on our own.

Cons

- Mom and Dad haven't met James' grandparents.
- I don't know if they will be with us or if they will let us be on our own at Disneyland.

Brock then got back on the phone and called James. "Hey, I just need a little more information for my parents. I know this might sound weird, but my parents don't know your grandparents. Are they good drivers? You know, they don't drink and drive or anything like that, do they? Yeah, I didn't think so since your parents are letting you go with them, but my mom's dad was an alcoholic, so that stuff is important to her. Oh, and will we be with them all day or on our own? Yeah, I kind of thought we'd be on our own." I smiled at Brock's candor and at the risk he was taking.

We ran down one last checklist of emergency scenarios:

"What if you get separated from James?"

"James and I will have an emergency meeting place where we can meet each other or his grandparents if we get separated."

"Do you have Dad's cell number memorized?" He reeled it off.

"What if you get up there and James was wrong and his grandparents have had alcohol with dinner?" He didn't like this question. He knew that if he said he wouldn't ride with them, then James would be offended. But he knew this was a deal breaker with us, and if he caved in and said he'd get in the car we'd say no. He stood silent for a moment.

"Brock, this won't be the last time you'll have to make this choice."

Then Bill and I each shared times we had and had not made the right choice in this area.

Brock finally said, "If I were a real friend, I wouldn't want James to ride in the car either if his grandparents were drinking. I guess I'd call home and talk over the decision with you two if that really did happen."

"Good answer. Sounds like a fun weekend—go for it."

The Treasure of Trust

Trust begets trust. Help your children build trust with you as they become teens. Surround your teen with many voices that echo the whisper of the Holy Spirit. The treasure of trust is complete when you no longer lead your child—God does.

Don't overreact. Your teen will be more likely to share information with you if you don't overreact. Trust can be hard for parents who love their kids. Take a deep breath if you need to before discussing a touchy situation.

Remember to thank your teen for a trustworthy act. One evening at the dinner table, Brock asked, "Friday night, Brandon wants a couple of us to spend the night. Here's why you should say yes: Brandon's mom will be there. We just want to hang out and maybe watch some movies. You know Brandon; I don't know if you've met his mom. Mom, since you have to fly out this weekend, I could take your car so if anything happened, I could drive myself home. You could talk to Brandon's mom on the phone ahead of time, Dad. I would still be home early enough Saturday to do all my work and homework. You know everyone who is invited."

Bill said, "Since I'm the one home this weekend, I'll call Brandon's mom, and if I like the answers I get, then you can go." Bill called, and everything seemed to be on the up-and-up. Bill did find out that Brandon's mom was a single mom, so he added a stipulation: "If any adults there are acting inappropriately, I want you to come home." Brock agreed.

After Brock had been gone about an hour and a half, Bill got a call. "Dad, can you come get David? With my provisional license, I can't drive with anyone else in the car. Some seniors showed up with a bunch of alcohol, and we want to leave. Can he come to our house and spend the night?"

"Sure. But where's Brandon's mom?"

"She's here. But she's in her room, and all she does is yell at Brandon to 'get those kids with that booze out of here.' Dad, Brandon keeps trying, but they won't go. We *all* asked them, and they won't leave."

Bill sensed the severity of the situation. He knew that either the seniors were just going to stay and be allowed to drink, or a fight could ensue, or the police would be called. All were negative options.

"Yes, I'll come right now. Meet me outside with all your stuff—"

"Dad, wait. Rodney's here too. He and a couple of the others want to leave, and Rodney said he'd drop off David at our place."

We knew Rodney. He was a Christian kid from a good family who lived a few blocks from us.

"Okay, and if you want all the kids to come over, Brock, they're welcome."

"Thanks, Dad."

Several kids stayed at Brandon's, not wanting to abandon him. But several came and hung out at our home. Bill and I were proud of Brock, and Bill complimented all the guys on making a right choice.

For the next few months, every time Brock asked permission for a privilege, he'd answer our questions, and I'd say, "Sure—you've been so trustworthy. You have a good head on your shoulders."

When you train, transfer, and trust, your children begin to see that those who honor God, God honors. Adults, teachers, and coaches compliment their character. Job opportunities, trophies, awards, and scholarships come their way. Their peers begin to come to them for wisdom. People seek them out as leaders for clubs and organizations. And one day, at a high school or college graduation, after a job interview, or at boot camp commencement, they will thank you. Or even more precious, your new son-in-law, daughter-in-law, or their parents will thank you for the job you did raising your child. At Brock's wedding reception, Zach, the best man, stood and gave a toast that included this phrase, "Our parents always taught us that those who honor God, God honors. And today God has honored you with a wonderful, beautiful, godly wife."

Decision Point
Transfer Trust

This week, practice saying words of trust. Instead of saying, "Don't do this," or "I better not hear you are doing that," try expressing what behavior you desire. For example, try something like this: "I know I'll hear a great report from that mom when she brings you home from the celebration." "I bet the coach will tell me what a leader you are at practice." "Your friends must really look to you for wisdom because you have such a good head on your shoulders." Speak the truth and speak faith into your children's ears, hearts, and lives.

How can you transfer an area of responsibility to your child? Consider the following contracts, and if you have a tweens or teens, have them complete the forms you think they are ready for.

My Relationship Contract

1. Read the verses below and in your own words write what you think they mean and what relational advice they give:

Genesis 2:24	Romans 8:5	Galatians 5:19
1 Samuel 16:7	Romans 12:1	Ephesians 4:22-24
Psalm 84:11	Romans 13:12-14	Ephesians 4:29
Psalm 139:13-14	1 Corinthians 6:18-20	Ephesians 5:11
Jeremiah 29:11	1 Corinthians 15:33	Philippians 4:8
Matthew 5:8	2 Corinthians 6:14	1 Thessalonians 4:3-6
John 8:32	Galatians 2:20	1 Timothy 4:12
John 10:10		

2. What traits do I hope to see in the person I someday marry? Which traits are nonnegotiable? (List internal traits, such as honesty, integrity, faith, financial security, empathy, and a sense of humor.) Which of these traits do I need to work on in my own life this year?

3. How will I know if the person I would like to date has those traits? (Below is a chart that will help you discern whether a person has the traits you are looking for. It will also help you identify negative traits.)

How Can I Decide?

Attributes	Green Light	Red Light
Character traits I want in the person I marry someday.	How can I tell the trait is there?	How can I tell the trait is *not* there?

4. How will my parents know I am ready to date responsibly? What things can I do in other areas of my life that will give them confidence to release me to spend time socially with those of the opposite sex?

5. Who is paying for my social life?

6. What transportation will I use for dates?

7. What kind of commitment will I extend to those I date? What does it mean to be boyfriend and girlfriend?

8. How will I assure my date's parents that their son or daughter is safe with me?

9. What do I need to talk about with my date's parents as our commitment grows? Am I willing to abide by their wishes?

10. What kinds of gifts will I accept and give and at what level of commitment? (Watch out for dates or gifts that up the intimacy level too early in the relationship. Remember, you have years to romance someone, so don't use all the tools in your first year! What gifts are less personal and emotionally safer to give earlier in a relationship?)

11. What are God's physical standards for my relationships at each stage? (Indicate which items on the following list are permissible at these stages: casual dating, serious dating, engagement, marriage.) First Thessalonians 4:3 makes it clear sex outside of marriage is off limits. Matthew 5:8 says, "Blessed are the pure in heart." Mark the list below in a way that will keep you pure in your heart, your actions, and your thoughts toward your date.

    • hold hands

    • hugs

- a kiss

- kisses

- make out

- petting outside clothes

- petting under clothes

- foreplay

- intercourse or oral sex

12. How and when will I communicate these standards and boundaries to the people I date?

13. What are safe places to date? (Active dates like bowling are safer than sit-around dates like watching a movie in the dark. List ten active dating options.)

14. What things will I *never* do on a date?

15. At what age will I be ready to...
    - group date (a bunch of friends together)
    - double date
    - single date

16. What is the purpose of single dating?

17. How much time will I spend with someone of the opposite sex? How will I know if I am spending too much time with someone?

18. What are my guidelines for talking on the phone, e-mailing, and instant messaging?

19. How will I respond if friends tease me for my standards?

20. Who can I ask to hold me accountable for my standards? (Choose leaders, mentors, best friends, or family members who intimidate you a bit! Also, choose people who can observe your life: a roommate, a youth pastor or mentor, a sibling, or a friend in your social circle—someone who can see and observe your life. Tell them your dreams and desires in the area of relationships, and ask them to hold you accountable for your choices.)

21. What are the consequences if I break my own conscience? (Consider setting new, higher boundaries, changing the places you go on dates, asking for more accountability, and even getting counseling if you continue to violate your own conscience. Continual failure may signal a deeper issue or problem.)

   - first offense:

   - second offense:

   - third offense:

Student's signature: _____

Parent's signature: _____

Date: _____

My Driving Contract

1. Who will schedule classes and driving tests?

2. Who will pay for a car, gas, insurance, and upkeep?

3. Who can be in the car?

4. Where can I drive and when?

5. What activities are allowed while I'm driving? (Eating? Listening to music?)

6. Who pays for tickets? What if I get in an accident or break my contract?

   - consequence for first infraction:

   - for second infraction:

   - for third infraction:

Student's signature: _____

Parent's signature: _____

Date: _____

My Work Contract

1. Where can I work? (How far from home? What kinds of jobs?)

2. How will I get there?

3. How many hours a week?

4. How will I use the money I earn?

5. What conditions must I meet to have a job, such as maintaining a good GPA and keeping up with my chores at home?

6. Consequences for violating my contract:

   - first offense:

   - second offense:

   - third offense:

Student's signature: _____

Parent's signature: _____

Date: _____

My Education Contract
(Junior High Through College)

1. What are my educational goals?

2. Where will I attend school? How will I make that decision?

3. How much does a college education cost? How much do I expect my parents to pay for?

4. What must I agree to do if my parents continue investing in my education? (Consider church fellowship, service and ministry, a minimum GPA, and social behavior.)

5. Consequences for breaking my contract:

   - first offense:

   - second offense:

   - third offense:

Student's signature: _____

Parent's signature: _____

Date: _____

TEN

Decide to Celebrate
Helping Your Child Recognize and Respond to God's Call

ᖇᖇᖇ

We were traveling with Caleb to the first social obligation of the day one Independence Day. Caleb asked for the third or fourth time, "Where are we going again?" I began to explain the list of stops we had planned for the day. Caleb interrupted and tried to list the events. He had them all wrong, so I said with a bit of exasperation, "Caleb, honey, you're not listening!"

"Sorry, Mom, I just mis-under-heard you!"

We both laughed, "That's great, Caleb! You are so right! People mis-under-hear all the time."

The one Person you want to make sure your children don't "mis-under-hear" is God. You want them to have the skills to listen to God's voice and His clear call on their lives. Effective parents pass the baton of faith and values to the next generation. They help children mature into the people God designed them to be. The most productive and fulfilled adults are those who have discovered and are living out God's unique call on their lives. When people find their passion, they are able to keep going and going and going. Life isn't a drudgery; it's a thrill and adventure.

Help Your Child to Communicate His or Her Faith

Children should have a platform from which to share Christ by the time they are 13. Adolescence will go smoother for those teens who have something they feel they are competent at, something that makes them feel special and visible, something that they value. But once they have that platform, how can they stand on it and share their faith?

A Little Bit at a Time

The best way to help children learn how to share their faith is to model it by sharing yours. Let your child see and hear your spiritual conversations. Let them see you serve God. Include them when you pray for those you would like to see come to faith in Christ.

When Brock was about five years old and on his first T-ball team, we prayed for each player on the team and his family. The prayers were simple: "Lord, we pray for Jimmy. Please help us show him and his family Your love. Please reach their hearts and introduce Yourself to them. Please let them come to You."

When Brock was 15, he was the master of ceremonies at the first Banquet of Champions sponsored by the Fellowship of Christian Athletes club he founded. As a part of the banquet, a professional athlete shared the gospel and gave an invitation to receive Christ. Jimmy prayed to accept Christ that night. Though many have come to faith in Christ through the many outreaches Brock and Zach have hosted, Jimmy's decision was special because our family had been praying for him for more than ten years.

Where to Begin

To help your kids find their niche and serve the Lord, give them a spiritual gift inventory, such as the Spiritual Gifts Questionnaire at www.elmertowns.com. Even more importantly, have them try lots of different things in ministry by volunteering in many different ways at church and in the community. Below is a sampling of spiritual gifts and some ways to use them.

1. *The Boss.* This person has gifts of leadership or administration (Romans 12:8; 1 Corinthians 12:5,28; 1 Timothy 5:17). Plan an activity, party, or event to tell people about Jesus or help people grow in their relationship with Jesus.

2. *The Artist.* This person has gifts of craftsmanship (Exodus 26:1; 28:3; 31:2-6; 35:10,25,30-35; 36:1-2; 38:22-23; 1 Chronicles 25:3; 2 Chronicles 20:21-22; 34:9-13; Acts 16:14; 18:3). Use your craftsmanship to create a project that is beautiful and that can be used at church or in your home to remind people about God, such as a banner, a cross-stitch, a woodworking project, or a painting.

3. *The Megaphone.* This person is an evangelist (Acts 5:42; Romans 10:15; Ephesians 4:11; 2 Timothy 4:5). Talk to someone about Jesus, invite a friend to church, or show someone your scrapbook and share your testimony.

4. *The Counselor.* This person has gifts of exhortation and wisdom (Romans 12:8; 1 Corinthians 2:1-3; 12:8). Listen to friends' problems and offer to pray with them. Try to find Bible verses that will help them.

5. *The Banker.* This person is a giver (Mark 12:41-44; Luke 18:12; Romans 12:8; 2 Corinthians 8:1-7). Give away money to help someone else. Give to a missionary, a needy family, a ministry, or your church.

6. *The Helper.* This person is gifted to serve (Mark 2:3-4; Luke 22:22-27; Romans 12:7; 16:1-2; 1 Corinthians 12:28; 1 Timothy 6:2). Work behind the scenes. Set up chairs, pass out fliers, make punch, pick up after Sunday school or youth group. Do something a janitor or a secretary might do!

7. *The Host or Hostess.* This person has gifts of hospitality (Acts 16:15; 21:16-17; Romans 12:9-13; 16:23; 1 Peter 4:9-10). Plan a party in your

home, or have friends spend the night and help them feel comfortable by letting them borrow your best things. Make something and take it to a neighbor or an elderly person and stay and talk a few minutes.

8. *The Prayer Warrior.* This person is gifted to intercede (Acts 12:1-17; 16:25-31; Colossians 4:12; 1 Timothy 2:1-8). Pray for 20 minutes for one person who is sick or hurting, pray out loud with someone who is sad, or pray for someone on your way to or home from school.

9. *The Brain.* This person is gifted with knowledge (Romans 15:14; 1 Corinthians 12:8; 13:8). Offer to use your brain power to help another. Try tutoring, or work in the sound booth, on a lighting crew, or on computers for your church or another Christian organization.

10. *The Nurse.* This person has gifts of mercy (Luke 10:33-35; Acts 9:36; 16:33-34; Romans 12:8). Help someone who is sick, disabled, or older or weaker than you are. Offer to work with special education children or children that need extra help in school.

11. *The Musician.* Musicians may be gifted to serve in many ways, such as evangelizing, encouraging, or leading in worship (1 Samuel 16:16; 1 Chronicles 16:41-42; 2 Chronicles 5:12-13; Nehemiah 12:27-40). Play in a church band or orchestra, sing in a choir, or play or sing a solo at church, in a nursing home, for the youth group, or at children's church. You might try writing songs about God to play for people who don't go to church and then find a place to play them at school or a public event.

12. *The Teacher.* Teachers have special gifts (Romans 12:7; 1 Corinthians 12:28; Ephesians 4:11; 1 Timothy 3:2). If you know one thing about Jesus, you know one thing more than someone else. Teach someone younger than you something you know about Jesus. Gather up some kids from your neighborhood, teach your younger brothers or sisters, or volunteer to help out in a younger classroom at church on Sunday or during the week.

13. *The Writer.* Writers share their gifts in words (Psalm 45:1; Acts 15:19-20; Philippians 3:1; 1 Timothy 3:14-15). Write something about Jesus and give your masterpiece away. Mail some handmade greeting cards, give your friends a short story or poem, or write a letter about an issue from a Christian point of view and send it to the editor of your local or school paper.

Let Them Help

My friend and the music director at our church, Debe, has helped her children share their faith in many ways. The first Christmas we lived in San Diego, I was discipling Debe. We decided we'd invite people to a Christmas party and include everyone in our families in some way. We wanted to share the gospel with our guests. We assigned her daughter Karly, then nine, the task of directing a Christmas pageant of the Christmas story with the cast of the children who came, including Brock and Zach, who were six and four, and her younger siblings, including Debe's baby, who would play the baby Jesus!

Karly stepped right up to the plate and created a wonderful drama with amazing costumes. The crowd wasn't very big that night, but little by little over the years, Karly was given more and more responsibility in dramatic presentations both onstage and behind the scenes. The audiences are much bigger now that she directs her own children's theater. She founded her children's musical theater to train children to share their faith through the arts. Her ministry has grown to include several groups, and she has traveled all around the world as a director and choreographer.

Party with a Purpose

One of the best ways to train children to share their faith is to entertain evangelistically. Children have many opportunities to party with a purpose: Christmas, Easter, before or after children's dramas, during a sports season, or in conjunction with a church event. Let's use a Happy Birthday, Jesus party as an example. This Christmas party can include the basic party ingredients:

1. *Welcome.* This is a great entry-level ministry opportunity—even a preschooler can hand out stickers, a nametag, or a candy cane to guests as they arrive.

2. *Icebreaker or game.* Every party needs entertainment. Simple games or crafts for young children, or icebreaker contests for teens, work well to make guests feel at home. This is a great second step for a child to take.

3. *A testimony.* A one-minute testimony of faith is a great start for a junior higher. This was the testimony Zach gave at his freshman football outreach:

> Many of you know Reggie White as the "Minister of Defense." That's his nickname. He was twice named Defensive Player of the Year and has been selected to the Pro Bowl 12 times! What is Reggie's source of strength? Why is he my favorite player? I can relate to him. When he was 13 years old, he went to church, and his pastor was a really cool guy. He liked what he saw in his pastor's life and found out it was Jesus. So he asked Jesus to come into his life then—and a personal relationship with God has been a source of strength for him ever since.
>
> My dad is a pastor, and I saw things in his life I liked too. One Father's Day, I told my parents I wanted to know God. I bowed my head and prayed and asked Jesus to come into my life, and He did. Since then God has been the source of my strength for many things—like trying new sports, meeting new friends, and for talking to you right now.

The next year at the freshman outreach pizza party, Zach added to this basic story:

> I used to be a pretty chubby kid. I was fat and unhappy, and my grades were bad. I was fifth string on the football team my freshman year. But through God's strength, I worked hard in practice, I stayed late, I lifted early, and in one summer I went from the fifth string in football to starting varsity. My grades are better—I am getting mostly As now.

If I can do it, you can do it, because God promises, "I can do all things through Christ who strengthens me."

When Brock entered high school and began having sports outreaches, he adapted his testimony to the audience. He began to grow in his ability to share his faith. Here's a sample of the testimony he gave at his football pizza party:

What do I have in common with Barry Sanders, John Carney, Mark Brunell, and Deion Sanders? Not football ability! It's that all these players and I have a personal relationship with Jesus Christ that gives each of us the strength and focus we need to succeed.

We're freshman now—and I have a challenge. I think we can be the winningest varsity team San Marcos has ever seen. I think we can be our personal best if we have three things: dedication, determination, and desire.

First, dedication. Play as a team. One of the first things I learned from God's playbook, the Bible, was "Do unto others as you would have them do unto you." We will play as a team when we think of the team and not just ourselves.

Second, determination. The Bible says those who know their God can do mighty things, and my favorite verse says I can do all things through Christ who strengthens me. God can help us work hard and not get distracted by things that can ruin our futures—like premarital sex, drugs, drinking, and fighting. God promises to be there for each of us no matter what. Danny Wuerffel is an example of determination. In 1996 he won the Heisman trophy and was named the College Hall of Fame Scholar Athlete. He credits his personal relationship with God as the motivating factor to this accomplishment.

Third, desire. It could be easy for us to say, "We don't have hot uniforms, and we don't have a new stadium." We could see ourselves as second-rate, but God doesn't see us that way. God made us, and He thinks we're first-rate—we just need to believe it and act like it! When I was just seven years old, I learned that God's desire was to help me be the best I could be, and I asked Jesus to come into my life. God has been keeping His promise to help me ever since.

Super Bowl veteran Eugene Robinson says, "Success is maximizing the opportunities where God has placed me." Today, you're going to hear about some opportunities that will help you maximize your potential, and I hope you'll take advantage of them.

4. *The gospel.* The final step is a simple gospel presentation. Following is a sample of the gospel presentation Brock gave:

God has a game plan for your life:

1. God loves you and offers you a wonderful plan for your life. Jesus said, "I came that they may have life, and have it abundantly" (John 10:10 NASB). Jesus also said that "God so loved the world, that He gave His only begotten Son, that whoever believes in Him shall not perish, but have eternal life" (John 3:16 NASB). What prevents us from knowing God and His game plan?

2. Man is sinful and separated from God. That's why people don't experience God's game plan for life. The Bible says, "All have sinned and fall short of the glory of God" (Romans 3:23). None of us, if we stood on a free throw line, would make 100 percent of the shots we take. God knew we were imperfect, so He came up with a plan to reconnect us to Him.

3. Jesus Christ is God's only provision for our imperfection. Through Jesus we can know and experience God's love and plan for our life. "God demonstrates his own love for us in this: While we were still sinners, Christ died for us" (Romans 5:8). Jesus said, "I am the way and the truth and the life. No one comes to the Father except through me" (John 14:6). But it's not just enough to know these truths.

4. We must each individually receive Jesus as our Savior and Lord. Then we can know God personally and experience His love and plan for our life. It's like we need to ask God to be our coach in life. "As many as received Him, to them He

gave the right to become children of God, even to those who believe in His name" (John 1:12 NASB). Jesus said, "Behold, I stand at the door and knock; if anyone hears My voice and opens the door, I will come in to him" (Revelation 3:20 NASB).

> Asking God to be the coach of my life is the best decision I've ever made, and as we end here I just want to pray out loud a prayer like the one I prayed. As I pray, if you want to make the decision to ask God to coach your life, then you can pray along with me silently.
>
> Jesus, thank You for loving me and offering me a great game plan for my life. I know I am imperfect and that You paid for that imperfection when You died for me on the cross. Please come into my life to be my Savior and Coach. Make me the kind of person You designed me to be. Thanks. Amen.

Pray for Your Child to Learn to Communicate His or Her Faith

Organizations like Child Evangelism's Good News Clubs, Student Venture, Fellowship of Christian Athletes, Athletes of Good News, Young Life, and many other church and parachurch youth groups give this kind of training. As your children join in these groups and step into the opportunities they offer, more opportunities will be opened up to them. Brock is asked to open our city council in prayer on a regular basis. Zach has been asked to lead Sunday school classes, and Caleb has hosted several Christmas and Easter outreaches for his friends and teammates and is currently interning to be a small group leader in the youth group.

What if your children are older and shy or reserved? Help them learn to use quieter ways to share the gospel. Have them write the family Christmas letter and ask them to include the gospel somehow in it. Have them create birthday or Christmas cards on the computer with a Scripture verse included in the well wishes. Ask them to play their instrument for the family Christmas gathering, and ask them to play a hymn or carol and then give out cards or gifts with a section of the lyrics attached. Make care packages for the homeless with God Loves You stickers on them. Pray, and God will give your entire family ways to share His love.

Help Your Child Discern God's Will and Hear His Call

Really, our purpose for writing this entire book has been to help you understand and recognize God's will for your child. But as a child gets ready to fly from the nest, the stakes go up. So what are some principles for knowing God's will?

What Is God's Will for Me?

The New Testament includes only a few statements that clearly say, "This is God's will," or "This pleases God." When we obey those statements, all our decisions will agree with God's will. We enjoy freedom when we obey the basic responsibilities God has laid out. Encourage your young adult to ask, am I...

Saved? "This is good, and pleases God our Savior, who wants all men to be saved and to come to knowledge of the truth" (1 Timothy 2:3-4).

Spirit filled? "Do not get drunk on wine, which leads to debauchery. Instead, be filled with the Spirit" (Ephesians 5:18).

Sanctified? "Therefore, I urge you, brothers, in view of God's mercy, to offer your bodies as living sacrifices, holy and pleasing to God—this is your spiritual act of worship. Do not conform any longer to the pattern of this world, but be transformed by the renewing of your mind. Then you will be able to test and approve what God's will is—his good, pleasing and perfect will" (Romans 12:1-2).

Sexually pure? "It is God's will that you should be sanctified: that you should avoid sexual immorality" (1 Thessalonians 4:3).

Saying thanks? "Give thanks in all circumstances, for this is God's will for you in Christ Jesus" (1 Thessalonians 5:18).

Suffering for right? "So then, those who suffer according to God's will should commit themselves to their faithful Creator and continue to do good" (1 Peter 4:19).

Seeking God? "Blessed are they who keep his statutes and seek him with all their heart" (Psalm 119:2).

Teach your children that if they walk according to God's principles, God will reveal His plan for their lives. God wants them to know Him, and as they do, He will be true to His promise that "whether you turn to the right or to the left, your ears will hear a voice behind you, saying, 'This is the way; walk in it'" (Isaiah 20:31).

What Spiritual Markers Do You Remember?

Often, by looking back, we can see how God has uniquely prepared us for our passion. Your child might have learned more than one language, lived in another culture, or received special training. God is also the master of turning a pain into a platform for ministry. The burning bush was a marker for Moses. He knew that God had spoken to him at a specific time and called him to lead His people even when he was hiding in the desert. Moses had other markers too. He was saved when Pharaoh was killing other baby boys. As he grew, he must have asked, "Why me? Why was I saved?" He was educated in Egypt. Who in all of Israel would have been better prepared to speak to the ruler but someone raised in the palace?

God places markers—clues—in every life, and as we look for them and help our children see them, we learn how to focus our lives. God built markers into your children's lives for a reason. He will direct their path.

Have your young adults complete the following exercises for more insight into their own calling:

1. *What are my successes?* Have them list their top five favorite or most meaningful moments of achievement.

2. *What is my uniqueness?* What does your child do in a unique or outstanding way? Os Guinness writes in his book

The Call that we need to replace "We are what we do" with "Do what we are."[1]

3. *What are my markers?* Have your kids write five to seven sentences about times when they gave their lives away—when they focused on others—and they felt, "Wow! That went well! I think I helped someone!" Then review those sentences and look for common threads. Maybe the people your kids ministered to are a certain age or in a certain circumstance. Or maybe they helped people by participating in certain activities like research, design, or taking care of things like computers.

4. *What are my gifts?* Many spiritual-gift tests are available, but the best way to discover a gift is to serve God in many ways and then look for a response, outcome, or validation. Often, people who know us best will compliment us when we are exercising our gifts. Help your young adults by listing compliments others have said about them to you. Or go one better: Ask those adults who are most important to your teens to speak or write their observations.

5. *What is my passion?* Ask your young adults what they would do for no pay just because they love it so much. Discuss questions like these: "If you had a magic wand and could change one thing in the world, what would you change?" or "If you could do anything for God, money was no problem, and you were guaranteed success, what would you want to do?" If they live out their passion in their career, work will never feel like work to them.

Help Your Child by Letting Go

Carol Kuykendall, author of *Give Them Wings*, reminds us that the task of adolescence "is to separate and gain independence; to pull away and find an answer to the question, 'Who am I, apart from this family?'" In my (Pam's) book *Got Teens?* (coauthored with Jill Savage), we describe a Freshman Foundation, a set of key questions in five vital areas of life: fitness, friends, future, finances, and foundations. (For a sampling of questions you can include in your family's Freshman Foundation, visit www.masterfulliving.com.)

When we walk through these questions, we try to set aside five days to do something special with our graduating senior. Brock went with us to a family camp on the Oregon coast, and we took a walk along the beach each day to discuss these areas. With Zach, we talked during five special dinners spread out over a few months. The final one was in his new hometown after he had moved into his own apartment. The important point is to talk together, ask questions, and listen to the answers. Your questions help your kids to think through some of the most vital life questions, and in doing so, they take even more responsibility for the life you have helped them mold. They find the key to their own future.

Carol Kuykendall shares a story of the day her teen son came home with an earring in his ear. She was wise enough not to overreact. Instead, she asked herself some vital questions:

> Retaining total control is not my goal in dealing with an adolescent. My aim is to empower that adolescent by giving him control that enables him to make his own decisions. So I try to clarify the conflict in my mind: Is this an issue about who is in control or about a boy wearing an earring?...Why is this issue bothering me so much? Do I want him to change his appearance for my benefit...or his? Is this my problem or his? Is this issue morally threatening or life threatening?...Am I allowing him to express his opinion?[2]

This separation is not easy for the parent, nor does it feel natural—but it is vital. I can count on one hand the number of times Brock has been in any kind of conflict with me, but mini episodes of "digging his heels in" seemed to happen with more frequency when he was nearly 17. I suddenly was hearing, "Okay, okay" when I asked him to do something, or "All right, Mom," with a bit of an attitude when I reminded him of a deadline or responsibility.

But when I affirmed how much I loved him and that I was encouraging him to take more responsibility for his own life, he said, "I know, Mom, I love you for helping me succeed."

We have heard those words on several occasions: the day we put Brock on the plane to Liberty University, the day we piled Zach's furnishings into a U-Haul to move to the University of Louisville, and the day we attended Caleb's eighth-grade award ceremony and watched him receive the Christian character award for the ninth year in a row. At Brock and Hannah's engagement party, we gave Brock a symbolic set of apron strings, showing we were releasing him. And most recently, we heard these words on the day Bill preformed Brock's wedding ceremony. After we prayed for him, he hugged us both and said thanks.

Those words are about the sweetest words a parent will ever hear. And you will hear them too. Some children give them liberally and early in life when they realize what a treasure proactive parents are. Others will have to become parents themselves to realize what a treasure their parents' love is. Because our children are so precious to us, we do want them to succeed in life—in the big things and the little things—and to become everything God designed them to be. Pay close attention to your map (God's Word), hold tightly onto your key (faithful prayer), follow your treasure-hunting Guide (the Holy Spirit), and you will successfully unlock the treasure inside your child one good decision at a time.

Decision Point

Mark a New Beginning

We make our choices and our choices make us. What parenting choices is God calling you to make? Is He asking you to fortify, adjust, adapt, change, or improve something in your own life? Look at the list of key parenting decisions below and select one area to begin working on:

1. Decide to be a positive, proactive parent: Do you need more information about a stage of your child's development or a struggle he or she is having?

2. Decide to be consistent: How do you need to change to better facilitate your kids' character development?

3. Decide character counts: What traits do you want to pass on as a legacy, and how will you do that?

4. Decide to have a plan: What is your family motto? What phrases or truths do you want to make sure your children grasp?

5. Decide to be creative: Do you need to pray, seek a professional, or read a practical resource to uncover the treasure inside your child?

6. Decide to be a student of your child: What adjustments in your parenting will bring out the best in each of your children? How can you enhance their gifts or personality? How can you help them by identifying their learning style or love language?

7. Decide to partner with God: Are you praying as a couple, with friends, and with your child?

8. Decide to build a network: Do you have a plan for your child in pain or your prodigal? Who can help you prevent pain or poor choices on the part of your child? Who can you team with to rescue, resource, or restore them?

9. Decide to trust: How will you transfer responsibility to your child in each area of his or her life, including the spiritual, financial, social, educational, vocational, and relational?

10. Decide to celebrate. How can you celebrate the great decisions and choices your child has already made, your child's unique personality and calling, or the transitions on the road ahead?

Long-Distance Loving

As your children mature, you will need new ideas to stay emotionally connected to them in a new, more adult friendship role. Here are a few:

- Keep a supply of picture postcards from the hometown area on hand for quick, one-liner messages.

- Clip articles of interest from the newspaper or send the sports section.

- Send a few family photos with captions.

- Send church newsletters.

- Send a tape or CD you've enjoyed. Record one yourself.

- Have a little brother or sister draw a picture.

- Write some "Proverbs from Home," starting with Proverbs 32, as the Bible stops at 31. This is a good way to tuck in some advice.[3]

- E-mail photos or prayers for their day, or have automatic e-mail greetings or thoughts for the day sent from Christian Internet sites that offer these options.

- Send money, stamps, or a gas or phone card tucked in a letter. (They may call to say thanks!)

- Invest in a timeshare, cabin, or other recreation activity that you and your young adult children and married children would enjoy with you.

- Send gifts of encouragement and applause. We were newlyweds when my husband graduated from seminary. My mother sent Bill a new white shirt and tie for "all those Sundays ahead."

- Send comfort gifts: Mom sent me Grandma's cookies and candies or brands of products I used growing up, like Avon hand cream.

- Care packages: I received a birthday in a box from my mom when I was away at school. I had all the ingredients for a cake, popcorn, candy, and streamers. There was always enough for a party in the care packages. Friends in my dorm were always happy to see my mom's packages arrive!

- Create a quilt out of all their award T-shirts. We gave this gift to Brock for his twenty-first birthday. It was a prayer quilt, and each person at the quilting party said a prayer and then tied a knot to secure the quilt. (This can also be a quilt made from their clothes while growing up or from their various uniforms.)

Group Discussion Questions

෴

Chapter 1—Decide to Be a Proactive Parent

1. What was or is your biggest fear as a parent?

2. Review Hannah's story (pages 12–14). Hannah told God that if He gave her a child, she'd "give him to the LORD." What does giving your child to the Lord mean to you? How would this look in today's culture? Have you prayed a similar prayer?

3. Hannah kept her word—she had personal integrity. Pages 14-15 list traumas caused by lapses in a parent's integrity. Did you experience any of these as a child? If so, what was the impact on your life?

4. What is something positive you learned from your parents that you hope your own children learn from you?

5. What are some things you'd like to change about the way you are raising your kids?

6. Have you experienced any answers to your prayers for your kids? If so, which stands out in your mind?

Chapter 2—Decide to Be Consistent

1. Children are born innocent or sinless. Their lives are like blank slates. Do you agree or disagree? Read Psalm 51:5.

2. This chapter lists five negative traits children would rather have than character. At what age do children usually begin to display these tendencies? How have you seen one of these characteristics manifested when your kids were very young?

3. What theme or principle runs through the verses on pages 41? Read the following verses as well: Psalm 6:1; Proverbs 5:23; 13:24; 22:15; 23:13; 29:15,17; Jeremiah 30:11; Ephesians 6:4; 1 Timothy 4:8; 2 Timothy 3:16-17; Hebrews 12:5-11; Revelation 3:19.

4. After reading those verses, how do you feel about spanking? Should discipline ever take a physical form? (Try to back up your opinion with a verse.)

5. Read the description of appropriate discipline on page 33. Are any of these items new for you? Which one do you want to make sure you remember?

Chapter 3—Decide Character Counts

1. What is the most important thing your child can own by the time he or she is 18?

2. Complete the chart on page 48. Share your chart with another group member and see what you had in common and what you might have forgotten and want to add.

3. How will you decide whether both parents will work—and how many hours?

4. How will you choose babysitters?

5. Review the lists on pages 51-55. What new thought or criteria will help you make educational choices for your children?

6. Write a one-paragraph prayer or a letter to your children to read when they are 18. Share it with the group.

Chapter 4—Decide to Have a Plan

1. What endears a child to your heart?

2. Review the Farrels' three main goals for their children. Try to write a one- or two-sentence mission statement that includes your parenting goals. Share it with the group.

3. Complete the Learner and Leader chart on page 66 for at least one child. Note how you feel as you work through it and when you complete it.

4. Review pages 68-70, and plan a Learner and Leader Day or a Summer Seminar. Share your ideas with the group.

5. What do you want your grandchildren to write about you?

6. Which are your favorite motivational tools and ideas on pages 77-80?

Chapter 5—Decide to Be Creative

1. How did you choose your children's names?

2. What creative idea has God given you that helped one of your children through a tough day or season?

3. How can Mom and Dad work in partnership? Does one parent in your family have more influence on the children than the other? How can you involve the other parent more? (If you are a single parent, how can you find someone of the opposite gender to help encourage your children? The group can help brainstorm ideas.)

4. Who are the people you look to for parenting advice?

5. Parents have to choose their battles with their kids wisely. What are some nonnegotiables for you?

6. Pam created a treasure map for Zach. How can you encourage or motivate your children? What have you or someone you know used to get kids in action?

Chapter 6—Decide to Be a Student of Your Child

1. What encouragement or compliment did you receive as a child that has left a lasting impact?

2. Fill in the blanks below for one of your children:

    A. Gender: _____

    B. Personality type: _____

    C. Birth order: _____

    D. Learning style: _____

    E. Love language: _____

3. What new insights did you learn about your child?

4. What changes do you want to make as a result of this information?

5. How can you share this information with your child in a way that will encourage or equip him or her?

6. How can you build your child's self-esteem?

Chapter 7—Decide to Partner with God

1. Write your current prayer concerns for your children on a 3 x 5 card. Exchange the card with another group member so you can pray for each other's children in the coming week.

2. In what ways can prayer help you as a parent?

3. Have you ever had to lean on God because of a crisis in your children's lives? Share your story with the group.

4. In prayer, have each person in the group thank God for one of His character qualities that has been a blessing to him or her.

5. Share one prayer request for your children, and pray for the person on your right.

6. Finally, take turns reading Psalm 91, personalizing it as a prayer for one of your own children.

Chapter 8—Decide to Build a Network

1. What is one thing you hope your children never say to you?

2. What special-needs child has had an impact on your family?

3. What can you do to encourage or support a parent of a special-needs or prodigal child?

4. Who would you call if you received bad news concerning one of your children?

5. What principle impacted you the most from this chapter?

6. What are your children's best traits, and how can you focus on their positives this week?

Chapter 9—Decide to Trust

1. Read the verses on pages 166-167. What is one benefit of walking in God's will?

2. By the time kids are 13, they should have something that makes them feel really great about themselves. How can you discover and nurture a talent or skill in your children?

3. What new thought or parenting skill stood out in this chapter on teens?

4. What decision-making tool for teens impressed you the most? How can you train your teen to develop decision-making skills?

5. How can you learn to trust your child (especially if he or she is already a teen)?

6. What is one benefit of having a teen complete the various contracts in this chapter?

Chapter 10—Decide to Celebrate

1. If your child were to give you a report card on your ability to live out the Christian life, what grade do you think he or she would give you?

2. What area of faith is strongest or easiest for you? What is a weakness or more difficult? How can you strengthen that area in your own life?

3. How can you involve your children in ministry or volunteer work?

4. Which of the spiritual gifts listed on pages 195-197 do you see in your child?

5. How can you prepare yourself to let go? How might you celebrate a young adult's transitions, such as graduation, going away to college, moving to his or her own apartment, entering the military, or getting married?

6. Share your favorite way to show love or encouragement to an adult child.

Recommended Resources

꩜꩜꩜

Personality

CLASS
PO Box 66810
Albuquerque NM 87193
(Offers a very inexpensive personality test)

Christian Financial Concepts
PO 2377
Gainesville GA 30503
(Offers Career Direct / Life Pathways to help your children decide on major and career)

DISC Test Personality Insights
PO Box 28592
Atlanta GA 30358

The Delicate Art of Dancing with Porcupines: Learning to Appreciate the Finer Points of Others by Bob Phillips (a resource book on temperaments, behavior styles, and social styles). Regal Books, Ventura, California.

Spiritual Gifts Inventory

Church Growth Institute
PO Box 7
Elkton MD 21922

Books

Got Teens? by Pam Farrel and Jill Savage
Celebrate! I Made a Big Decision by Pam Farrel
The New Birth Order Book by Kevin Leman
Unlocking Your Child's Learning Potential by Cheri Fuller
The Way They Learn by Cynthia Tobias
Answering the 8 Cries of the Spirited Child by Dave and Claudia Arp

Organizations

Family Life Today
3900 N. Rodney Parham Rd.
Little Rock, AR 72212

Focus on the Family
Colorado Springs, CO 80995

Hearts at Home
900 W. College Ave.
Normal, IL 61761

Masterful Living
Pam and Bill Farrel
PO Box 1507
San Marcos, CA 92079

Moms In Touch
PO Box 1120
Poway, CA 92074-1120
Phone: 800.949.MOMS or 858.486.4065

MOPS (Mothers of Preschoolers)
PO Box 102200
Denver, CO 80250-2200

Parent Talk
PO Box 3700
Tucson, AZ 85740

NOTES

༺࿇༻

Chapter 3—Decide Character Counts

1. Brenda Hunter, *Where Have All the Mothers Gone?* (Grand Rapids, MI: Zondervan, 1982), pp. 92-93.
2. Ibid., p. 90.

Chapter 4—Decide to Have a Plan

1. Available from Mom's Jar of Preserves Company, 991 C Lomas Santa Fe #435, Solana Beach, CA 92075.
2. Many thanks to Pam, Esther, Kristi, Tammy, Michele, Maria, Kristina, Tracey, and Jay—all wonderfully creative moms!

Chapter 6—Decide to Be a Student of Your Child

1. Sheila Brownlow, Rebecca Whitener, and Janet M. Rupert, " 'I'll Take Gender Differences for $1000!' Domain-Specific Intellectual Success on *Jeopardy*," *Sex Roles*, February 1998.
2. Ibid.
3. Florence Littauer, *Raising Christians—Not Just Children* (Dallas, TX: Word, 1988), p. 73.
4. Ibid., p. 54.
5. Kevin Leman, *The New Birth Order Book: Why You Are the Way You Are* (Grand Rapids, MI: Revell, 1988), p. 15.
6. Ibid., p. 16.
7. Ibid., p. 18.
8. Ibid., p. 187.
9. Cynthia Tobias, *The Way They Learn* (Colorado Springs, CO: Focus on the Family, 1994), p. 19.
10. Ibid., adapted from pages 91-96.
11. Gary Chapman, *The Five Love Languages of Teenagers* (Chicago, IL: Northfield Publishing, 2000), p. 127.
12. Ibid., p. 128.
13. For "Caught You Being Good" stickers, contact More Hours in My Day by calling Sheri Torelli at (909) 682-4714.

Chapter 7—Decide to Partner with God

1. Stormie Omartian, *The Power of a Praying Parent* (Eugene, OR: Harvest House, 1995), p. 14.

Chapter 8—Decide to Build a Network

1. H. Norman Wright, *Loving a Prodigal* (Colorado Springs, CO: Chariot Victor, 1999), p. 50.

2. Gleason Archer, *Encyclopedia of Biblical Difficulties* (Grand Rapids, MI: Zondervan, 1982), p. 253.

3. Cheri Fuller and Louise Tucker Jones, *Extraordinary Kids* (Colorado Springs, CO: Focus on the Family, 1997), pp. 26-28.

4. Ibid., pp. 33-34.

5. Ibid., p. 38.

6. Wright, *Loving a Prodigal*, p. 53-54.

Chapter 9—Decide to Trust

1. Dave Arp and Claudia Arp, *Suddenly They're 13 or the Art of Hugging a Cactus* (Grand Rapids: HarperCollins, 1999), p. 67.

Chapter 10—Decide to Celebrate

1. Os Guinness, *The Call* (Nashville, TN: Word, 1998), p. 46.

2. Carol Kuykendall, *Give Them Wings* (Wheaton, IL: Tyndale, 1994), p. 62.

3. Ibid., p. 157.

More Great Harvest House Reading from the Farrels

ᦓᦓᦓᦓ

Got Teens?

Jill Savage and Pam Farrel offer commonsense solutions, insightful research, and creative ideas to help you guide your children successfully into adulthood. You will discover biblical advice, support, and encouragement for your journey.

The 10 Best Decisions a Woman Can Make

Bestselling author Pam Farrel encourages you to exchange the fleeting standards of the world for the steadfast truths found in a growing, fruitful relationship with God as you find your place in His plan.

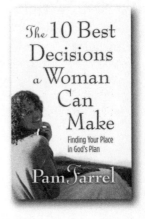

Men Are Like Waffles—Women Are Like Spaghetti

The Farrels explain why a man is like a waffle (each element of his life is in a separate box), why a woman is like spaghetti (everything in her life touches everything else), and what these differences mean. Then they show you how to achieve more satisfying relationships. Biblical insights, sound research, humorous anecdotes, and real-life stories make this book entertaining and practical.

Single Men Are Like Waffles—Single Women Are Like Spaghetti

Helping waffles and spaghetti understand and relate better to each other, the Farrels explore the "Way of the Waffle Warrior," the "Plight of the Pasta Princess," and "Waffles, Spaghetti, and Kids." A helpful discussion guide is included.

～～～